D1562415

PRAISE FOR
TIMELESS: 10 ENDURING PRACTICES OF APEX LEADERS

Apex leaders usually don't know they are apex leaders. Others notice them, study them and write about them so leaders like me can read, learn and grow. My friend, Brian Dodd, has made it easier for me in his book *TIMELESS: 10 Enduring Practices of Apex Leaders*. You, too, can become an apex leader and even develop others to do the same. See you at the apex.

DR. SAM CHAND
Leadership Consultant and author, *Bigger Faster Leadership*

Brian is a student of leaders and the art of leadership. In *"Timeless: 10 Enduring Practices Of Apex Leaders"*, he has given us all the gift of distilling decades of learning from other leaders and packaged so we can apply it to our lives. This would be a perfect resource for you and your team to go through together ... it would generate so many great conversations to take your people to the next level in their leadership. Thanks Brian for helping so many with this resource!

RICH BIRCH
Founder, unSeminary

I have known Brian for 30 years, and he sees all of life through the lens of a leader. His insights did not come to him over a cup of coffee and a few minutes with a white board. These come from a lifetime of leadership and keen observations of leaders. You will recognize these principles as the title says: *Timeless*. Brian is a master illustrator. The stories he uses bring clarity and makes the principles stick. But what I like most are the questions at the end of the chapters that will help as I lead my staff in walking through these pages. This practical book will be a permanent part of your library.

MARK MARSHALL
Senior Pastor, The Glade Church, Mt. Juliet, TN

I am so glad Brian Dodd has taken the time to pen this book, Timeless: *10 Enduring Practices of Apex Leaders.* For years, Brian has penned daily leadership blogs that have challenged and inspired me in leading others. I agree with the practices that he outlines in this book and found myself nodding constantly all throughout! You will enjoy reading this book, and you will be thrilled if you put into practice what he wrote.

DR. BRIAN STOWE
Senior Pastor, First Baptist Church, Plant City, FL

Not only is Brian Dodd one of the most encouraging people I have ever met, he is an amazing student of leadership. He recognizes it in all walks of life and brings those principles in focus for the church. The character traits he identifies in this book are worthy of reflection and discussion. I highly recommend it for you and your entire team. Read it together!

MICHAEL LUKASZEWSKI
Founder and CEO, Church Fuel

Leadership is a gift, but it's also a stewardship. When it's stewarded well, it produces immediate results and lays the foundation for a long-term legacy. Because of that, leaders also crave the honest truth. What gaps exist in our leadership? Where do we need to develop? Leaders never settle, and this book will challenge you and the people you mentor to take your next steps in growing your influence.

TONY MORGAN
Founder and Lead Strategist, The Unstuck Group

We all have leaders that we follow, respect, trust, and learn from. There have been incredible leaders throughout history. Brian helps you see what they have in common and how to learn from their example. I thoroughly enjoyed this read and think every Christian leader would be remiss to not invest the time to learn from Brian's work.

GREG ATKINSON
Author and Founder, First Impressions Conference

Some people build companies, some build organizations, some build churches; Brian Dodd builds people. Within the pages of *Timeless: 10 Enduring Practices of Apex Leaders*, Brian shares ten practices from within the trenches of leadership. Stories, principles, lessons learned, characteristics, and timeless practices that, if applied, have the potential to turn you (or any reader) into an Apex Leader.

JT TERRAZAS
Lead Pastor, Hope City Community Church, El Paso, TX

Brian Dodd has more than just observed the lifestyle of generosity; the words he writes are born out of the way he lives. He has unwittingly sparked many revolutions of generosity and challenged many Christ-followers to 'live original' with their time, talents, and ever controversial-treasure. Brian's knowledge of generosity is both wide and deep, and supports the foundation that when Christ is the richest of all treasures, everything else is given appropriate value. Reading his book emulates watching a leadership forum: ESPN-style. Do your heart and mind a favor and plug him in!

REV. R. KEVIN CROSS
MST, EA, CPA*, NTPI Fellow®, Pastor, Communicator,
Counselor, and Fraud Lecturer

As is so often his custom, Brian Dodd is right on the mark in *Timeless* with his identification of essential traits in Apex Leaders! His rich, value-laden examples capture how many of the world's most notable leaders conduct their business and invest in the people around them. This read is so directly applicable for leaders serving across many different organizations and levels, it an indispensable part of any personal or professional library. I can't wait to share *Timeless* with others in my organization!

DR. BRIAN V. HIGHTOWER
Superintendent of Schools, Cherokee County, GA

In *Timeless*, Brian Dodd provides incredible insights into the challenges and goals of leadership. The discussion questions alone are worth the price of this book! You will be encouraged with practical and useful knowledge that can and will transform your leadership.

KURT BUBNA
Senior Pastor, Eastpoint Church, Spokane, WA

Do you want to grow as a leader? Look no further! *Timeless* will challenge you, convict you, and compel you to reach your maximum potential. Great leaders are always looking for practical ways to take their influence to the next level. Brian exemplifies what it means to be an Apex leader, and this book will give you a compass on how to become one!

DANIEL LUCAS
Lead Pastor, Better Life Church, Morehead, KY

Brian Dodd is one of the finest purveyors of leadership today, and his new book, *Timeless,* is a must have for every leader. It will be a book you read again and again in your own quest to become an apex leader.

JUSTIN TRAPP
Founder, Sermonary.co

Brian has become a trusted and valued source for leadership insight in my life. With the release of his new book, Timeless, we see the culmination of a tremendous amount of research and diligence to bring key leadership practices to countless leaders including you!

FRANK BEALER
Executive Director of Leadership Development, Orange/The rethink Group

There are plenty of leadership "experts" out there today, but when I look for unique insights about being a leader, Brian Dodd is my first call. His new book is a treasure chest I'm keeping on my desk because I need to be reminded of these principles every day. There are plenty of leadership trends out there, but if you're interested in the ideas that never change, and endure through a shifting culture, then get your hands on this book. It's the kind of resource that will change the way you think about leadership.

PHIL COOKE, Ph.D.
Filmmaker, media consultant, and author of *The Way Back: How Christians Blew Our Credibility and How We Get it Back*

This book is awesome!!! Here's what you need to know about Brian Dodd: He not only loves leaders, but he's also a practitioner. The dude knows what he's talking about. Brian has become a great friend, and I'm glad to recommend *Timeless: 10*

Enduring Practices Of Apex Leaders. I get asked all the time what separates the best leaders from everyone else. *Timeless* will give you the answers. If you want to become the best leader possible, make sure you get a copy for yourself and everyone on your team.

PERRY NOBLE
Founder, The Growth Company

Brian Dodd is an observer of people and a world-class miner who extracts the wisdom from every encounter he experiences with others! In other words, Brian does the hard work of distilling what distinguishes transformational wisdom from just informational wisdom in those who succeed at a high level. In Brian's latest book, *Timeless: 10 Enduring Practices Of Apex Leader,* he formulates the qualities that set apart leaders with character which makes them an Apex Leader in Brian's mind. Buy the book, read the book, apply the book, and you too can reach the apex of your Leadership potential!

DR. DWIGHT "IKE" REIGHARD
Senior Pastor, Piedmont Church, Marietta, GA

I have found in life that there are those that write about leadership and just observe traits. Then there are those that read about leadership and mimic others thoughts. However, in every generation there is someone who 'gets' leadership and intuitively understands what makes the great leaders tick. Brian Dodd is that guy. This book is a great blend of spiritual leadership and fabulous stories from high achievers! This book lays the groundwork as we all strive to be Apex Leaders!

MIKE LINCH
Senior Pastor, NorthStar Church, Kennesaw, GA

Timeless

10 Enduring Practices of Apex Leaders

BRIAN K. DODD

Timeless: 10 Enduring Practices of Apex Leaders

Published in the United States by NIN PUBLISHING – Anderson, SC

Printed in the United States of America
Signature Book Printing, www.sbpbooks.com

Cover design by Megan Hibbard

Edited by Rachel Rivers

Library of Congress Control Number: 2017919610
Dodd, Brian K.
ISBN 978-0-692-04562-6
First Edition

To my daughter Anna:

You are one of the great future Apex Leaders in Christianity. May you generously use your gifts, talents, and abilities to make the world a better place.

TABLE OF CONTENTS

FOREWORD

For a book to be written, the author must feel it has to be written. It sounds strange, but it bears repeating. The author feels the book has to be written. He or she has something to say which needs to be shouted from the rooftops. Maybe the author has discovered a certain truth they want to share. Perhaps he or she has developed a solution to the problems plaguing a portion of our society or a system that relieves suffering, fixes an injustice, or improves the quality of human life. The author may even need to tell the story of a great individual or team who accomplished much by overcoming significant adversity. These are the reasons a book has to be written. More specifically, these are the reasons a leadership book has to be written.

These narratives are so compelling to me that they caused me to experience personal discontent and sleepless nights. After completing my first book, *Ten Indispensable Practices of the Two-Minute Leader*, I did not have anything else burning in my heart to say to a larger audience. Of course, there were things I was interested in: apex leaders, leadership lessons from the Bible, churches helping the poor and under-resourced, and churches deeply investing in marketplace leaders in their congregations. I was interested in all of these topics but not fully committed to any one idea. I did not have a second book to write — until now.

Apex Leaders are a concept I discussed in my first book. When you think of the term "Apex", words like "zenith," "summit," "peak," and "greatest" may come to mind. Apex Leaders have reached the pinnacle of their profession. These individuals are recognized for excellence in their area of discipline and have achieved many of its highest rewards. In short, Apex Leaders are the best at what they do.

I have been deeply interested in Apex Leaders for over a decade, and I wondered what made them unique. Why do they stand out? How do they prepare? How do they think? Is replication of these great leaders possible or did God simply tap a few select people on the shoulder and ordain them for greatness? These were answers I had to know.

Over the last decade, I have read hundreds of books and articles on Apex Leaders. This information has provided me vast amounts of behavioral data on which I have written extensively. In fact, I identified an astonishing 307 different qualities, behaviors, and practices by these collective individuals. For example, some included fundamental traits such as joy, courage, contentment, humor, and feelings of freedom.

Out of these 307 identified qualities, ten of them rose to the top as the most common. These ten practices are unique to those at the top of their profession. The wonderful news is both you and I can implement these ten practices as well. These practices are not just for a select few. They are not just for the privileged, the resourced, or the relationally connected. I believe God has also tapped you on the shoulder for greatness!

What are these practices? Before we begin, let me introduce the greatest leadership book ever written that discusses Apex Leaders: the Bible. The truths contained in its pages provide instruction on practical leadership items like money management, conflict resolution, team building, personal boundaries, strategy, exercising and yielding to authority, communication skills, and character issues like honesty and personal pride.

The Bible's central figure is Jesus Christ. In my first book, I describe him as the perfect leader. In that book, I outline the qualities found in the Bible that show practical ways Jesus demonstrated supreme leadership during his life on earth. In 1980, I met this perfect leader, and I've been following him ever since. I have seen confirmation in my life and the lives of others that the leadership principles in the Bible and of Jesus are timeless.

As I prepared to write this book, this is the question I sought to answer: Are the timeless truths of the Bible reflected in the behaviors of modern-day Apex Leaders? This is a compelling question because not every Apex Leader is a Christ-follower. In fact, many Apex Leaders do not seem to follow a moral compass at all.

However, I discovered the ten most common practices of today's Apex Leaders, regardless of spiritual influence, were the exact same ones followed by the great leaders we read about in the Bible. The apostle Paul once wrote to Timothy, a young leader he was developing, "All Scripture is given by inspiration of God, and is profitable for doctrine, for reproof, for correction, for instruction in righteousness, that the man of God may be complete, thoroughly equipped for every good work," (2 Timothy 3:16-17).

The Bible is practical and applicable to all areas of a leader's life. With this in mind, I have used each chapter to unpack Scripture, so we can gain a proper context of the leadership journey of biblical leaders. We will also connect to modern practice by learning lessons from current Apex Leaders from the religious, athletic, nonprofit, and business sectors. You will walk away with practical tools you can use immediately to improve your leadership.

As you read this book, you may wonder about certain behaviors and practices that did not make the Top 10. Courage, decisiveness, preparation, patience, compassion, and character are certainly distinctives of great leadership. While those are embedded in my research, they are not always necessary to become an

Apex Leader.

However, those behaviors and practices are necessary to remain an Apex Leader, especially when it comes to character. Becoming and Remaining. The relationship is simple. There are times when a leader's talent can take them to places where their character cannot sustain them. We have seen this over and over throughout history. Corporate misconduct, oppression, thirst for power, domestic abuse, incompetence, lust, and greed are certain to derail a leader's influence. These actions have taken down countless high-profile leaders. This book focuses on the achievement side of this equation. It outlines the practices needed to reach the pinnacle of your profession.

I hope you will find the following pages to be challenging, inspiring, and sometimes counter-intuitive. If you follow these ten practices, there is no doubt you will become a better leader. These truths are available to everyone, not just a select few. However, only a select few choose to apply them. They are Apex Leaders. I hope you become one of them.

May God bless your journey!

— Brian

CHAPTER 1
Apex Leaders Build Great Teams

Then God said, 'Let us make man in Our image, according to Our likeness" (Genesis 1:26a, NASB)

The most common trait of all the Apex Leaders I studied is this: they build great teams around them. Apex Leaders have an intuitive sense that what they are called to do is so significant, so impactful, and so life changing, there is no way they can accomplish it alone. Therefore, Apex Leaders carefully select a group of individuals possessing skills that they personally lack.

Jesus Christ was the greatest leader who ever lived. He was the greatest vision-caster. Jesus was the greatest communicator and public speaker. No one has ever balanced compassion and difficult decision-making better than Jesus. Jesus is the model of perseverance, creative thinking, and courage, and no one has ever built a more impactful and enduring organization than the local church.

One of the reasons the local church has thrived is because a group of men hand-selected by Jesus, through the power of the Holy Spirit, went on to turn the world upside down. This team Jesus selected became known as his disciples. But as impactful as the disciples would later become, they were not on Jesus' greatest team.

The greatest team Jesus was a part of has existed for all of eternity. He is actually still part of this very same team today. God the Father, God the Holy Spirit, along with Jesus, God's Son, make up the team known as the Trinity. Each person in the Trinity has unique responsibilities. The Trinity also provides the model for how all teams should function and operate. Let me explain.

The Trinity demonstrates the purest form of unity and sense of community. There is no competition, jealousy, arrogance, demanding of rights, grudges, or walls erected between the three.

The Spirit does not demand attention but rather shines the spotlight on Jesus. Put simply, one of the primary ministries of the Holy Spirit is to glorify Jesus.

Jesus, likewise, is all about others. He did not come to be served but to serve (Mark 10:45). He said to the

Father prior to his crucifixion, "Father, if it is your will, take this cup from me; nevertheless not my will, but yours, be done" (Luke 22:42). The Father points to Jesus as well. He said after Jesus' baptism, "This is my beloved Son, in whom I am well pleased" (Matthew 3:17).

Each member of the Trinity serves, points to, and glorifies the other members. John Ortberg says, "The Father loves and glorifies the Son. And the Son submits to the Father and the Son says, 'It's a good thing the Spirit is going to come.' And the Spirit comes and points people back to the Son. It's an endless Trinitarian fellowship of love and joy and delight with each other. That's what's real. It's the most real thing in all of existence."

Ortberg calls the Trinity, "The Core of Reality." The Core of Reality for Apex Leaders is they are part of selfless, humble teams who are committed to each other's success. When success comes their way, the individual team members consistently shine the spotlight on others. Harry S. Truman famously said, "It is amazing what you can accomplish if you do not care who gets the credit."

John Elway, the two-time Super Bowl champion and Hall Fame quarterback of the Denver Broncos, told *Sports Illustrated* in a January 12, 2015, article, "When I realized I'm not the one who has to do it all that [is

3

when] we started winning championships. I threw for 120 yards (in Super Bowl XXXII) and we won. I was like, I don't care! I did my job!"

Part of a leader's job is to build great teams. One such leader is Jeffrey Neal, the chief marketing office of Kforce. He told *Inc.* magazine in 2016, "Think about what propels companies from the startup stage to something truly significant. At the heart of the matter, it is all about your people. Who you surround yourself with makes all the difference." Your team is your primary difference maker.

Jurgen Klinsmann
One team that was a primary difference maker was the 2014 United States Men's National Soccer Team. Generally considered the greatest team in U.S. men's soccer history, head coach Jurgen Klinsmann gave a glimpse into the team building process in a *USA Today* article published on June 28, 2016.

It is important to understand that people are always a reflection of their leader. Show me a bad team, business, church, or organization, and it can almost always be traced back to a bad leader. The inverse is true as well. Show me a great team and I can almost always trace it back to a great leader. The 2014 U.S. men's soccer team was no different. They reflected Klinsmann's personality and approach to soccer.

Building   a   great   team   requires   improving

performance and upgrading talent. Klinsmann completely overhauled the U.S. roster. Only six players remained from the 2010 World Cup roster. This required making hard decisions and courage. He decided Landon Donovan, the most decorated player in U.S. soccer history, should no longer remain on the team. As unpopular as the decision was, it proved to be the correct call.

Coach Klinsmann feared Donovan would become bigger than the team itself. This ran against the culture Coach Klinsmann hoped to create. Veterans would make the squad but only those who put the team first. Coach Klinsmann clearly defined the expectations for veteran players such as goalie Tim Howard and captain Clint Dempsey. Everyone played a role and stayed within the team concept. No one rocked the boat. The team had no stars (at least in Coach Klinsmann's eyes).

Building a great team requires an investment in talented young people. NFL Hall of Fame general manager Bill Polian often said he wanted his team "green and growing." Coach Klinsmann added eight players under 25 years old to the World Cup team. These eight players would form the nucleus of the 2018 and 2022 World Cup squads. Young talent ensures a successful and sustainable future. I have heard Dr. Ike Reighard, senior pastor of Piedmont Church, say, "If you can't hire the best, hire young."

He went on to add that young leaders may take more time to mentor, but this is offset by energy, excitement, and enthusiasm.

When building a great team, you should also look for under-valued and undiscovered talent. Great teams are often made up of individuals other people miss. Midfielder Kyle Beckerman played only 10 matches for the U.S. team from 2007 to 2009. Fellow teammates Mix Diskerud, Omar Gonzalez, Graham Zusi, and Chris Wondolwoski played a combined 11 matches entering 2013. They became part of the team's core.

Finally, Coach Klinsmann teaches us that courage is required in building a great team. You must be willing to make corporate sacrifices. Coach Klinsmann's approach to leadership was to make "the decision to sacrifice one for the good of many." You must also make personal sacrifices. Klinsmann conducted several controversial interviews regarding his team's limited chance of success. While heavily criticized by the media, he put the pressure on himself rather than his team. Whether you lead a church, business, nonprofit or sports team, when you lead in the area of sacrifice, you are modeling what is needed for success.

Apex Leaders have also learned a deeper truth about team building. There is a stark difference between hiring someone who works for you and hiring someone who works with you regardless of where he or she falls on the organizational chart. Hiring someone who works for you refers to acquiring an individual with a certain skill set needed to accomplish an assignment or task. Working with someone is much deeper. It refers to partnership.

Apex Leaders are looking for partners when they seek out prospective team members. They want to work *with* people. How do you know the difference? When hiring prospective team members, I look for the following:

Skill Wise leaders apply a team member's skill to a specific task. Everyone is not treated the same. The breadth of assignment is determined by a person's skill. The more skill a person has, the more assignment she will receive. Conversely, the less skill a person has, the less of an assignment she will receive.

Work Ethic This is not to be confused with "die trying." Just because a person gives great effort does not mean they have a proper work ethic. Work ethic refers to focused energy. Someone with excellent work ethic determines that something "can be done" and then gives focused, targeted, strategic time to "getting it done." They will not spend time on what cannot be done. If a leader is going to spend time on something, they will get it done!

Passion Passion means accepting nothing less than success. It is focusing on the right things, not all things. Passion is not broad, but it is deep in its focus. It forces a leader to choose between good and best. Passion results in an approach that is both specific and strategic. Passionate leaders make a choice and then own the results of their decision.

So, if you need to develop a talent acquisition strategy, begin with skill, work ethic and passion.

What happens if you only have two of the three qualities?

Skill + Work Ethic – Passion = Independent Contractor

This person bets on himself. There is seemingly little loyalty to the organization. He or she often provides their services to the highest bidder. For many people like this, work is nothing more than a job or short-term assignment to them. They last for only a season. While they may be profitable for a short period of time, you cannot build a lasting organization with independent contractors.

Skill + Passion – Work Ethic = Wasted Effort

These individuals are talented and motivated. They have bought into your organization's mission and

8

vision at a deep level. Everything is left on the field. They give you a lot of effort. However, their effort and good will are not being leveraged toward tasks which move the bottom line. They have confused activity with accomplishment. You often hear the following said about this sort of person, "He looks busy but nothing seems to ever get done."

Passion + Work Ethic – Skill = Rudy

The movie *Rudy*, which chronicles the journey of Notre Dame Fighting Irish walk-on football player Rudy Ruettiger, has inspired millions. Apex Leaders, however, are conflicted when they watch the film.

We are inspired by Rudy's work ethic, perseverance, sacrifice, passion, and the physical price he was willing to pay in order to play football for Notre Dame. While those are all qualities Apex Leaders hope to find in their employees, a struggle exists because if you have a team full of Rudys, you will lose every game. There is simply not enough skill to win. Apex Leaders would rather have players who dominate Rudy each day in practice while also having passion and work ethic. Give me those players and I will give you a national championship team.

Apex Leaders look for all three when building a team — Skill, Work Ethic, and Passion.

9

Nick Saban

For a modern-day example, few leaders understand effective teambuilding better than Nick Saban, the legendary head football coach of the Alabama Crimson Tide. From 2008 through 2017, the Crimson Tide had the nation's top recruiting class eight times. The other two years they had the second and fifth-rated classes. There are no Rudy's on Coach Saban's team.

As Coach Saban was coming up through the coaching ranks, he had the opportunity to be the defensive coordinator for legendary head coach Bill Belichick and the Cleveland Browns from 1991 to 1994. Posted in the Browns' office was the statement: "We are not in the talent collection business. We're in the team building business." This is a philosophy Saban has always espoused. Regardless of what type of organization you lead, you must build a program and insert people into your system and structure, not just collect talent.

Whenever I speak with competent church or business leaders and they mention a certain team or department is under-achieving, a deeper look often reveals they were simply collecting talent and not building a team.

All of Coach Saban's teams basically look the same–large offensive and defensive lineman, great running backs, skilled wide receivers, tall cornerbacks who play man-to-man defense, safeties who can support the run, and efficient quarterbacks who limit mistakes. This is because he has a system. He knows what he is looking for and is able to plug those individuals into his program.

Building a great team around you allows you to have margin. Margin allows you freedom. Freedom allows you to pursue the dreams God has put in your heart.

As you lead the team you have assembled and pursue your God-given dream, you quickly learn that achieving it requires a character trait we will discuss in the next chapter — humility.

Personal and Group Discussion Questions

1. What is one thing you learned about teambuilding from the leadership of Jesus that you can immediately implement?

2. List all of the members of your team and rate them on their skill, work ethic, and passion. How do they display these qualities on a daily basis?

3. Bill Belichick had a sign in his office that reads, "We are not in the talent collection business. We're in the team building business." Do you have a documented system for the type of individuals you are looking to hire? If so, explain. If not, take a moment and outline the type of person who best fits your organization.

CHAPTER 2

Apex Leaders Are Humble

Pride goes before destruction, a haughty spirit before a fall.
(Proverbs 16:18, NIV)

Luke 19:1-10 gives the intriguing account of an interaction between Jesus and a man named Zacchaeus.

Zacchaeus was a chief tax collector for the Roman government and consequently, became very wealthy. On a daily basis, he had tough conversations, made hard decisions, and had great responsibilities. He managed large sums of money and probably reported to some of the most influential officials in the land. I think of him as a modern-day department head for the Internal Revenue Service.

He was possibly at the top of his profession. He probably had the finest living arrangements. His future was likely quite secure. Money can buy many things, but conversely, there are also many things money cannot buy.

Zacchaeus realized no amount of money could buy happiness or contentment. Money could not buy peace, respect from others, satisfaction, significance, or a quality family life. Most importantly, no amount of money could satisfy his soul.

Tax collectors were hated. They were Jewish people who were hired by the Roman Empire to tax their own people. Tax collectors could collect as much money as they desired, and after paying the government their share, could then keep the extra for themselves. This was legalized extortion. Zacchaeus was not simply a tax collector but the chief tax collector. In Jericho, the city in which he lived, Zacchaeus was quite possibly one of its most despised individuals.

But there is a transition statement in verse 3 which changes the narrative. Luke records that Zacchaeus, "sought to see who Jesus was." Why? Why would the most hated person in a city want to meet Jesus? I propose that despite his incredible professional success, Zacchaeus despised his job. He hated waking up on Monday mornings. Every trip in public held the possibility of a confrontation with someone he had extorted. His professional relationships were with evil businessmen. Stress was a constant unwelcome companion. His health was possibly being affected by his job, and it probably had a negative impact on his family as well.

It is my feeling Zacchaeus spent his entire career climbing the corporate ladder, and when he reached the top rung, he discovered the ladder was leaning against the wrong wall. Something inside him told him there was more to life, more to leadership, and more to his career than extortion, greed, and constant unhealthy conflict.

Zacchaeus had heard about Jesus. The miracles, the healings, how he treated people, the taking on of the establishment, and his loving personality were attracting the largest crowds anyone had ever seen.

He had probably also heard about a fellow tax collector named Matthew, who 15 chapters earlier left the same profession to follow Jesus. Can you imagine the shockwaves Matthew's decision sent throughout the tax collecting community? Despite the pay cut, the word on the street was that this was the best decision he ever made. Jesus had changed his life and given it meaning. Matthew was having the time of his life and Zacchaeus was humble enough to think the same thing could possibly happen to him.

It takes a lot for a grown man to admit their chosen path in life isn't working out. For Zacchaeus, this was not a simple career decision. It was not "I don't think I like tax collecting anymore. I'm thinking about going into IT work." This was not a midlife crisis. For him, this was much deeper. He was desperate to find meaning and a greater purpose to his one and only life.

Upon arriving along the path Jesus was walking, Zacchaeus encountered another hurdle. He was vertically challenged. He was short, and his height was causing a problem. Because of the size of the crowd, he could not see Jesus.

I imagine Zacchaeus trying to fight through an unaccommodating crowd. The crowd was likely in a fanatical state to see Jesus, and Zacchaeus was being physically pushed aside. Perhaps people recognized Zacchaeus and saw this as an opportunity for payback. It was as if a portion of the crowd had bifurcated feelings. Most were focused on seeing Jesus but some turned their focus to Zacchaeus and basically said, "You're on our turf now little man!" They were not going to allow him to pass by, or it was simply a large crowd and Zacchaeus could not get through to see. I imagine watching him hopelessly jumping up and down to no avail. Whatever the reason, Zacchaeus was being reminded of his inadequacies.

Zacchaeus was reaping what he had sown. As a Jewish man, he was undoubtedly familiar with the famous saying found in Proverbs 16:18: "Pride goes before destruction, and a haughty spirit before a fall." Most experienced leaders have a level of sympathy for this first century chief tax collector because they have been there themselves. They have learned that pride is such a foolish personality trait. In addition to leading to destruction, it has already been established that you cannot accomplish anything great alone. Zacchaeus was in the crucible. He was in the process of becoming a broken and humble man.

In Jewish culture, it was shameful for a grown man to run in public, but Zacchaeus put his pride aside for a chance to meet Jesus. He ran to a sycamore tree, scaled it, and saw the One who would ultimately change his life.

Two thousand years after Zacchaeus fought through a crowd, former Louisville Cardinals head basketball coach, Rick Pitino, wrote in his book, *The One-Day Contract: How To Add Value To Every Minute Of Your Life*: "The lesson of humility comes to everyone eventually. Either you learn its value, or life drills it into you — and life can be a painful teacher." As an aside, I would add to Coach Pitino's comments that success and prosperity mostly turn to out to be terrible teachers.

C.S. Lewis famously said, "True humility is not thinking less of yourself; it is thinking of yourself less." Robert Herjavec, the business tycoon seen on the ABC hit series *Shark Tank*, quoted his mother in July/August 2016 edition of *Inc.* magazine, "Nobody in this world is better than you, but you are no better than anyone else." Leading from a position of humility is necessary for anyone wanting to reach the apex of her profession.

Apex Leaders consistently break down barriers between themselves and their teams. They proactively remove hierarchical forms of leadership and create cultures where everyone is treated the same. They get on same level as the people on their team.

For instance, Intel CEO Paul Otellini told *Glassdoor.com*, an organization who gathers information on employee feelings and executive compensation, "There is no differential treatment; the CEO to the RCG—all sit in similar cubicles and are provided the same resources."

Zappos, Inc.
Another organization that encourages humility in its leaders is the online shoe and clothing retailer Zappos. This highly successful organization is profiled in Joseph A. Michelli's wonderful book, *The Zappos Experience*. As I read Michelli's account, I learned much about the power of humility.

Humility is a difference-maker. It gives your church, business, nonprofit, or athletic organization a competitive advantage. Zappos has a collaborative and diverse culture — aggressively tearing down walls between people.

Humility allows you to serve customers more effectively. You think less about short-term profits and more about long-term relationships. The company's user experience (UX) team is made up of active listeners who are well-informed through market research and given the freedom to do trial-and-error in satisfying their customers. Michelli notes, "Business can be, and increasingly must be, about the development of personal relationships that span a customer's lifetime. While average managers might think a company can thrive simply by selling goods or services to customers, true leaders understand that all business is personal."

Since Michelli mentioned the word "leader," let's go there. Humility can be leveraged as a leadership strategy. Zappos employee Rhonda Ford said, "Tony (CEO Hsieh) and the other leaders have always treated us as equals. We are all Zappos. Leaders have never been too self-important to pick orders or to run across the warehouse so the customer's item makes it on the delivery truck. We follow the leadership's example of dedicated effort."

Finally, humility is simply more profitable. Michelli concludes, "Companies that truly allow staff members to take care of the best interests of customers enjoy, on average, more than 20 percent greater profits than those that operate from a less customer-centric perspective."

Humility also helps Apex Leaders in other areas. In the September 2013 edition of *Inc.* magazine, GSATI CEO, Cindy Tysinger, told the story of being forced to borrow money from family during a difficult financial stretch. Being humble and asking others for help was a key to surviving this difficult time.

Humility also helps you earn respect. Prior to becoming the Most Valuable Player of the 2016 Super Bowl, Denver Broncos linebacker Von Miller was still a developing athlete as a second year player in 2013. It was then he told *Sports Illustrated* in a January 19, 2013, article, "I feel I've taken steps in that direction (earning respect), but I still have a long way to go."

But most importantly, humility makes those you lead successful. While appearing on the June 22, 2016, *Herd With Colin Cowherd* radio program, Casey Wasserman, CEO of the sports marketing and talent management organization The Wasserman Group, said, "Part of being the boss is putting your ego and your issues aside and being the sounding board for everyone else's. It's about creating the right culture and that culture is about creating an environment for people to be successful and do what they're best at and that usually means putting your stuff aside and embracing theirs."

Stephen Curry
Few professional athletes model humility better than Golden State Warriors point guard Stephen Curry. During his 2014-2015 Most Valuable Player acceptance speech, he made the following quotes:

- "First and foremost, I want to thank my Lord and Savior Jesus Christ for blessing me with the talents to play the game, with a family to support me day-in and day-out."
- "I'm his humble servant right now."
- "I can't say enough how important my faith is to how I play the game and who I am."
- "I'm just blessed and thankful for where I am."

These four quotes teach us several things about Curry and other humble leaders. They do not deny their talents but are thankful for them. Humble leaders acknowledge that no matter how good they are, they are in constant need of support. All successful leaders must be servant-leaders first. They acknowledge they have been granted opportunities not for personal gain, but for the betterment of others.

After reading Curry's words, I propose to you that

humble Christian leaders should understand authority better than leaders who are not Christ-followers. This is a strong statement, but it is because they know what it is to both exercise authority as well as be under authority. Humility is realizing all your talents, gifts and abilities come from God and humbly serving him with your life.

Humble leaders are often self-deprecating, having an "Aw shucks, what me?" approach to life. This is not false humility. They are simply trying to be good stewards of gifts they realize they do not deserve.

Humble leaders are often well-prepared because they know "they are not that good." Ironically, humility increases a leader's confidence. Sir Laurence Olivier was once asked what made him such a great actor. He said, "The humility to prepare and the confidence to pull it off." As a result, humble leaders, not alpha dogs, are often top producers.

Humble leaders have longevity. They put the needs of others ahead of their own and the mission of their organization ahead of their personal agendas. Humble leaders are polite. This allows them to develop mutually beneficial, long standing relationships. They are well-liked and a pleasure to be around. Rarely does arrogance and pride yield a long shelf life.

Humble leaders bring stability to your organization

by bringing a sense of calm to those around them. They never seem rushed or panicked. Everyone around them has a sense of security. They communicate everything is going to be fine. Humble leaders are also eternally optimistic.

Vin Scully

When I think of a modern-day, humble Apex Leader, few are as recognizable as Los Angeles Dodgers announcer Vin Scully. For 67 years, he was the voice of the Los Angeles Dodgers. The man affectionately known as "The Voice of Baseball" is not so much a baseball announcer, but rather a poet who just happens to announce baseball games. Scully is a true Apex Leader. He is the GOAT (Greatest Of All-Time), a cultural icon, and he is deeply beloved by the sporting community and all who know him.

Heading towards his retirement at the conclusion of the 2016 season, *Sports Illustrated* writer Tom Verducci profiled the Dodger legend in a May 10th, 2016 article. Scully concluded their time together by saying, "I'm not only getting this job to do a sport that I love, but then God's charity allowing me to do it for 67 years...It's overwhelming, I mean, I have a big debt to pay in heaven—I hope when I get there—because the Lord has been so gracious to me all my life."

Do you have a big debt to pay in heaven? I suspect

you do. The Lord has been gracious to you as well. Are you ready to put your ego aside like Zacchaeus, the team at Zappos, Stephen Curry, and Vin Scully?

This is why humble leaders are so hard to find. Humble leaders know they have not arrived. They know they need to get better. The mission and vision of what they are trying to accomplish is too important to remain the same.

Leading from a position of humility allows you to implement the next truth—the need for continual improvement.

Personal and Group Discussion Questions

1. Would those you lead describe you as humble? Why or why not?

2. Proverbs 16:18 says, "Pride goes before destruction, and a haughty spirit before a fall." Explain the implications of this verse for your leadership.

3. Explain how increased position, money, success and influence over the course of your life and career have affected you.

CHAPTER 3

Apex Leaders Continually Improve

… his father rebuked him and said to him, "What is this dream that you have had? Shall I and your mother and your brothers actually come to bow ourselves down before you to the ground?" (Genesis 37:10, NASB)

There are several sure-fire ways parents can raise spoiled children. They can treat them as if their happiness is all that matters. Parents can shield them from suffering, pain, and the consequences of their actions. These children are made to be the stars of the family and are continually recognized for all they do. Do you know anyone like this?

When we meet Joseph in Genesis 37, we find the picture of a spoiled child. He was his father's favorite son and as a result, a despised brother. His coat of many colors was a constant reminder to all who knew him of his preferential treatment. Joseph made things even worse with his brothers by being a tattletale and braggart.

It is true Joseph received a dream from God that he would eventually reign over his brothers, but there was a significant difference in maturity between the person with the dream and the person in the dream. Joseph was brash, impulsive and unwise. His early life teaches us that maturity is not something that can be assumed. It can only be developed through the crucible of brokenness. Joseph would have to be broken.

It is in brokenness that a leader learns: "I'm not all that." To be used as a leader by God we must die to our sin and realize there is a significant gap between where we are and where God needs us to be. This gap can only be filled by God himself.

All leaders will experience brokenness. It is not a question of if, but when. Either the world will break you or God can break you. The difference between the two is that the world moves on to the next leader without remorse, but God rebuilds you into someone better than before. Are you willing to be rebuilt? If so, you could possibly become an Apex Leader marked by continual improvement.

Brett Favre
Brett Favre is one of my all-time favorite football players. Spanning a 20-year Hall of Fame career, I have never seen a professional athlete compete with

the joy and passion Favre did. This is why his final season with the Minnesota Vikings was so difficult to watch.

On December 10th, 2010, Chicago Bears defensive end Corey Woutton, lined up to blitz the Viking quarterback. At the snap of the ball, Woutton sped past left tackle Bryant McKinnie and slammed Favre to the ground with such force it left him unable to play for the team's final three games of the season. Favre's Hall of Fame career concluded with the legendary quarterback injured and sitting on the bench.

All leaders should watch Favre with a warning label saying: "Caution." The sobering reality is that any leader, at any moment, could become painful to watch. Those we report to will say "Thanks for serving our organization so well. We wouldn't be here if it wasn't for you" as security ushers us out the door with our pictures and awards in a cardboard box.

Apex Leaders constantly improve. If you are not focused on continual improvement, here are just some of the reasons you may need to get your cardboard box ready.

Technology will pass us by if we do not stay up-to-date on the latest trends and innovation. One of the places this shows up most in a competitive economy is with young people entering the workforce. Younger people are often simply bigger, stronger, faster, and often smarter than those who've been around for awhile.

Young people sometimes think older people are out of date, and they may be right. Conversely, older leaders may dismiss younger ones because of their appearance, habits, and inexperience. A leader does this to his own demise. Pride and arrogance are enemies of continual improvement.

Complacency is an enemy to continual improvement as well. Some people choose not to prepare like they once did. Even worse, they may stick out their chest and say the six words all leaders whose best days are behind them have said, "I've heard all of this before." Lasting leaders have learned what made them successful today will not keep them successful tomorrow.

Continual improvement is also needed because of leadership transitions. All leaders are temporary employees. A person may lead for two years or forty years, but eventually every single one will exit their leadership role and hand the reigns to someone else. This new leadership can arrive with a new vision and direction for the organization. Because they did not hire the existing staff or have any emotional attachment to the team, they may move on to the next individual if the current team has allowed themselves to become stagnant.

Continual improvement is often needed not because leaders or those who report to us change, but because they do not. Familiarity can become an enemy to a leader. Our message can become stale. They have heard all our stories, seen all our motivational techniques, read all our fireball emails, and can imitate us down to a T. We must remain fresh to get the most of our teams. People want to follow curious and evolving leaders.

When I think about Favre, what saddens me, as a fan, is it appears he stayed too long simply because of his love of the game. Apex Leaders rarely walk away too early. They are passionate individuals who give their organizations everything they have. However, Father Time is still undefeated. Every leadership position is temporary. Continual improvement will extend the assignment, but eventually there will come a time to hand it off to the next person.

While self-preservation is a strong motivator for continual improvement, there are several additional reasons continual improvement is needed:

There is a life cycle to everything. Change is inevitable and the older a leader gets, the harder it is to stay relevant. An Apex Leader never asks, "Am I part of this organization's past?" but, "Am I going to be a part of the future?" Continual improvement assures sustainability and continual options.

Current Apex Leaders may also one day serve the next Apex Leader who can bring out our very best. Continual improvement allows us to be prepared.

We are not owners of our careers, merely renters. Let's handle them with care and leave our positions and organizations better than we found them.

Brett Favre did that. He provided fans with many enjoyable Sundays and great memories. Favre left the game better game than he found it. But the game still moved on, and so will all organizations without continual improvement.

Roger Penske
Roger Penske is the owner of the auto racing group Team Penske, the Penske Corporation, and many other automotive-related businesses. He is one of the corporate directors at General Electric and was chairman of Super Bowl XL in Detroit, Michigan. Penske was previously on the board of The Home Depot and Delphi Automotive before resigning to chair the Detroit Super Bowl Committee. He had an estimated net worth of $1.95 billion as of September 2015.

Brad Keselowski, one of his team's drivers, noted in a May 26, 2016, *USA Today* article that Penske has an insatiable "pursuit of growth." He added, "Roger's ability to grow intellectually, personally, and his desire to do so has not leveled off over time, and I think that makes him an exceptional person by today's standards."

What is fascinating about Keselowski's thoughts is that Penske was 79 years old when those comments were made. Penske has lived a life devoted to personal growth. He has never stopped learning, never stopped growing, never stopped discovering new things, and never stopped improving. This is a primary reason why he became a billionaire. Penske is a reminder that it is never too late to improve.

Soccer superstar Lionel Messi told *Sports Illustrated* in a May 30th, 2016, article, "My goal is to constantly be improving. Year after year you can grow as a player, just as in life. You can always learn something new."

Think about that statement. The greatest soccer player of his generation stated his goal is not personal awards or championships. His goal is continual improvement. Year after year he is growing. Messi is always learning something new. Can you say the same?

Martin Luther King Jr. famously said, "If a man is called to be a street sweeper, he should sweep streets even as a Michaelangelo painted, or Beethoven composed music or Shakespeare wrote poetry. He should sweep streets so well that all the hosts of heaven and earth will pause to say, 'Here lived a great street sweeper who did his job well.'"

Have you ever met someone like that? I recently did. Her name was Gail.

Let me tell you a story about Gail.

Hampton Inn Employee Named Gail
Because of my work, I travel frequently, so I have stayed in my fair share of hotels. Not many hotel visits have stuck with me like the one when I met Gail. My family and I were visiting Lynchburg, Virginia, and Friday, July 1, 2016, started out like any other morning in a hotel.

We were headed out for the day, when I realized I left something in the room. My family waited in the lobby while I went back to the room to retrieve the item. As I exited the elevator and began walking down the hallway, I passed a lady from the cleaning and maintenance staff. The following conversation took place:

"Good morning," she said.

As I casually walked by, I responded, "Good morning ma'am. How are you today?" I wasn't really expecting a reply.

She said in an unusually joyful voice, "I'm great! How was your room?"

Surprised by the second question, I looked up and said, "It was very good. Thank you for asking. How is your day going?"

"It's going very well. I hope you have a blessed day."

"Thank you ma'am. I will. I hope you do as well."

I thought, "That is the nicest cleaning lady I have ever met." As I quickly grabbed a few things out of my room, I walked back past her cleaning cart towards the elevator and noticed a book entitled *Walking With Giants: The Extraordinary Life Of An Ordinary Man* written by Dr. Elmer Towns. If you are not familiar with Dr. Towns, he is the co-founder of Liberty University. He also authored more than 175 books on Christianity, prayer, and the church. Only heaven can truly record the impact of this man's life. His book was in this lady's cart and was obviously being read throughout the day.

When I arrived back down in the lobby I told the hotel manager and front desk personnel how nice this lady was. The manager said with a smile, "That's Gail. She's great!" to which I responded, "Yes, she is."

In my history of hotel stays, I have witnessed how

staff tend to spend their breaks. Most of them have not been reading leadership books.

Gail apparently spends her breaks reading books on personal growth. She is on her way to becoming an Apex Leader in her profession. It wouldn't surprise me to hear one day that she is leading the entire hospitality staff of the hotel chain.

This brief but impactful encounter reinforces several keys about continual improvement.

People who continually improve can make a BIG impact in someone's life in a very short period of time. My time with Gail was less than 20 seconds, yet I was immediately marked by her personality and desire for personal growth.

Another reason why continual improvement is so important is because of the impact it allows you to have. To be extraordinary all you need to do is be ordinary and provide a little extra. Ask the second question. Smile. During this particular trip, we also had two twin beds in our room. Gail could obviously tell which one my teenage daughter slept in. When I returned to the room her bed had an extra blanket. Just a little extra takes something from ordinary to extraordinary.

A simple thing all leaders can do to improve is read books. Right now, the lessons from this book are making you a better leader. King Solomon once wrote, "When the ax is dull and its edge unsharpened, more strength is needed, but skill will bring success" (Ecclesiastes 10:10). By reading this book you are sharpening your ax and increasing your skill. Great leaders are great readers.

Dr. John C. Maxwell often says, "Your attitude determines your altitude." Positive people simply have more options and become more successful. Let's use Gail as an example. I have encountered tens of thousands of workers in my life in hotels, restaurants, gas stations, banks, etc. Yet, I remember Gail because her attitude made her remarkable. Will your attitude help make your leadership worth remarking about?

Finally, continual improvement is important to your Christian witness. I have heard it said: Preach the gospel every day. Use words if necessary. You should easily be able to tell if a leader is a Christian or not. You should intuitively know whether or not a person genuinely loves Jesus. Gail did not have to tell me she was Christian. In fact, we did not discuss one spiritual item, but I knew about her faith after only eight words.

May we all approach life like Gail. May we also approach our careers and leadership like Gail. May we all have the ability to impact others like Gail, and may we preach the Gospel of Jesus Christ with our lives every day — and use words when necessary.

Continually improving leaders have strong work ethics. They never rest on their laurels. Continually improving leaders are constantly upgrading their skills and looking for new mountains to climb.

Continually improving leaders are humble (there's that word again) and have the self-awareness to know they can get even better. One way they do this is by simply getting smarter. Young leaders often rely on passion and energy. However, Apex Leaders know the value of life experience, industry knowledge, and accumulated intelligence.

Continually improving leaders eventually become experts at their craft. They play to their strengths. They prioritize their activities to achieve maximum results.

Leaders who continually improve move beyond positional titles to influence. At this level, they improve the overall performance of their entire organization. They become the rising tide which lifts all ships.

Above all, continually improving leaders become respected and wise.

Now let's look at leaders who have chosen the

opposite approach. Let's look at leaders who have made a conscious or unconscious decision to become complacent and satisfied. Let's look at leaders who thought they had arrived and had all the answers. The Bible calls leaders who refuse to continually improve foolish. These individuals can become entitled, arrogant, lazy, complacent, or misguided.

Proverbs 26 provides a profile of foolish leaders and how to deal with them.

Do not celebrate foolish leaders or give them honor. Verse 1: "… *honor is not fitting for a fool.*"

Foolish leaders lack self-discipline. Verse 3: "*A whip for the horse, a bridle for the donkey, and a rod for the backs of fools.*"

Foolish leaders have foolish conversations. Verse 4: "*Do not answer a fool according to his folly, or you yourself will be just like him.*"

Do not encourage foolish leaders. Verse 5: "*Answer a fool according to his folly, or he will be wise in his own eyes.*"

Do not trust foolish leaders with important information. Verse 6: "*Sending a message by the hands of a fool is like cutting off one's feet or drinking poison.*"

Foolish leaders lack skill and waste resources. Verse 7: *"Like the useless legs of one who is lame is a proverb in the mouth of a fool."*

Foolish leaders waste opportunity. Verse 8: *"Like tying a stone in a sling is the giving of honor to a fool."*

Foolish leaders have poor judgment. Verse 9: *"Like a thornbush in a drunkard's hand is a proverb in the mouth of a fool."*

Foolish leaders never learn or grow. They make the same mistakes over and over again. Verse 11: *"As a dog returns to its vomit, so fools repeat their folly."*

There is little hope for foolish leaders. Verse 12: *"Do you see a person wise in their own eyes? There is more hope for a fool than for them."*

Continual improvement is an absolute necessity to become an Apex Leader, and it will help you avoid being a foolish leader. The next quality will also help, and it is the one I find people struggle with the most.

Personal and Group Discussion Questions

1. As a leader, have you experienced true brokenness–something which has marked your life forever? If so, explain.

2. What steps are you currently taking to one day leave your current leadership position and organization better than you found it?

3. What one area of your life are you working on right now for your own continual improvement?

4. What is one thing you are doing right now to help foster a spirit of continual improvement within your team?

5. When you read the 11 qualities of a foolish leader listed in this chapter, how many describe you? What changes are you willing to make to begin the journey from certain foolish behaviors to wise ones?

CHAPTER 4

Apex Leaders Work Hard – Very Hard

You will eat the fruit of your labor; blessings and prosperity will be yours. (Psalm 128:2, NIV)

In my study of Apex Leaders, hard work was the second-most listed trait of people who reach the top of their professions. Hard work is one of my favorite subjects. It is a passion of mine. Hard work is something anyone can do, but only a few choose to do. Nothing of significance happens in a leader's life apart from hard work.

One of the teams I lead has a number of burgeoning millennial leaders. They are extremely talented and frankly, will one day pass me in many areas of leadership and influence. However, I currently have a two-decade head start on them. I often advise them, "If I'm ahead of you (experience, networks, contacts, wisdom, sales pipeline, etc…) and work harder than you today, you'll never catch me."

Apex Leaders Work Hard — Very Hard

Many leaders think their talent and competence alone will get them where they need to go, but hard work will always beat talent and competence when talent and competence don't work hard.

Sometimes it is smarter to work harder, but make sure you do not confuse activity with results. While you are working hard, always be on the lookout for new and better ways to complete the job.

One of my favorite leaders is Chuck Bengochea. In addition to being the former Chief Executive Officer of Family Christian bookstores and HoneyBaked Hams, Chuck is also a world-class Ironman contestant in his age category. Because I served under his leadership when he was the Chairman of the Elders for Fellowship Bible Church in Roswell, GA, he and I are great friends. Once I interviewed him for a business leaders' Bible study I was conducting and asked him about the subjects of hard work and perseverance. Chuck's words stunned all of us in attendance.

He said, "You can do an Ironman. You just have to persevere and choose to, on that day, spend a lot time in agony." Wow! Success is attainable, but it comes with a price. I have learned many people want the perks of leadership — the compensation, the notoriety, the material possessions, etc., but few are willing to pay the price of leadership. Hard work is one of the primary prices that must be paid.

Booker T. Washington once said, "Nothing ever comes to one, that is worth having, except as a result of hard work." In fact, the only place success comes before work is in the dictionary. Prior to winning a gold medal at the 2016 Summer Olympic games, swimmer Haley Anderson said in a June 14, 2016, *USA Today* article, "Some days, it does make me wish I was relaxing instead of putting in all this hard work. But if it wasn't hard, it wouldn't be worth it." Successful leaders understand the rewards of hard work are definitely worth paying the price needed for success.

The Bible has a lot to say about hard work. Allow me to give you just a few verses from Proverbs along with some key leadership lessons they provide.

If you do not work hard, you will not enjoy financial success. In fact, laziness provides a clear path to poverty. Read Proverbs 6:10-11 (NIV): "A little sleep, a little slumber, a little folding of the hands to rest—and poverty will come on you like a thief." Dave Ramsey, a financial expert, said, "My children were taught at an early age how money works and that it comes from hard work. They've been on a commission—not an allowance—since they were little. They learned that if they worked around the house, they got paid. If they didn't work, they didn't

43

get paid."

Are you looking for more meaning in your life and work? Do you want to lead something with meaning and purpose? Well, hard work brings leaders understanding and a sense of satisfaction. Proverbs 12:11 shares, "He who tills his land will be satisfied with bread. But he who follows frivolity is devoid of understanding." Failure to work hard is frivolous. In other words, without hard work, there is no serious purpose to your actions. Hard work provides direction and intent. Former British Prime Minister Margaret Thatcher summed it up when she said, "What is success? I think it is a mixture of having a flair for the thing that you are doing; knowing that it is not enough, that you have got to have hard work and a certain sense of purpose."

It may sound unusual to discuss this topic in a primarily Christian leadership book, but one of the many benefits to hard work is your quality of life. Proverbs 13:4 (NIV) teaches us: "A sluggard's appetite is never filled, but the desires of the diligent are fully satisfied." What do you desire today? Is it financial gain? Loving relationships? Physical, mental and emotional health? A great church, business, athletic organization or nonprofit? Do you want to be able to give away great amounts of time and resources to meet the needs of others? Whatever it is you want to be rich in, it cannot be accomplished apart from some hard work.

Many times people wonder why other people "get all the breaks." They wonder why someone else is in charge instead of them. Many times there is a very simple answer. Proverbs 12:24 teaches us, "The hand of the diligent will rule, but the lazy man will be put to forced labor." Successful leaders, who wind up in key positions of influence, do not talk about working hard. They do it. Abundant Life Christian Fellowship's senior pastor Bryan Loritts said during the 2014 Global Leadership Summit, "If the poor want to eat, let them come and work your field."

These verses are sobering. The contrast between hard work and laziness is not a popular topic in today's politically correct and entitled culture, but if you want to get the most out of your leadership, you need to know that success smells a lot like sweat. Thomas Edison once said, "There is no substitute for hard work." Baseball superstar Albert Pujols said, "When you're here, you're working. This is what gets you ready. If you want to have a championship ballclub, this is where it starts." These are lessons I know all too well.

As both a church volunteer and a member of a church staff, I did not always work hard. I worked hard compared to others, but I did not always give my absolute best. This truth hit me like a ton of bricks on a men's retreat in October 2000.

Several hundred of us from NorthStar Church in Kennesaw, Georgia, attended the two-day event on the campus of Berry College in Northwest Georgia. Berry's campus has a sprawling estate where, on any given day, you can pass dozens of wild deer on the way to classes and dorm rooms. The section we stayed in was called Camp Winshape. Winshape was started by Chick-Fil-A founder Truett Cathy and his wife Jeannette. It is the perfect place to get away from the hustle-and-bustle of the city and re-examine your life. The Winshape experience is also designed to build character. Little did I know how my two days there would "shape" the course of the rest of my life and leadership.

One of the character-building exercises on the property is a ropes course. This particular event requires you to climb approximately 30 feet up into one tree and then swing back and forth to another. At midnight, our group of approximately 25 men, all under the age of 35, began taking turns climbing the tree and leaping into the darkness. One by one we strapped on our harnesses and began our ascent.

I had a slight fear of heights but nothing that would prevent me from climbing 30 feet in a controlled environment. However, this was definitely outside of my comfort zone. When my turn came, I put on my helmet and began to climb: one foot after another. At about 20 feet, I stopped and inexplicably climbed back down. I made some joke about having a family and a mortgage and gave my helmet to the next person in line.

We were trying to get 25 of us through this exercise as fast as possible, so we could get back to our dorm and go to sleep. The others were probably happy my turn went quickly, but as I stood in the darkness, I knew the truth: I had tapped out. I went just to the point of pain and discomfort and then quit. I did not push through. I did not pay the price needed to achieve my objective. Those words are hard for any leader to admit, but the truth is clear–I quit.

But something more impactful was happening while I stood there alone in the dark. This character-building exercise revealed I had been a quitter not just in my attempt to climb the tree, but I had been a quitter for my entire life.

Eighty percent of church attenders do absolutely no volunteer work. As a church volunteer myself I should get points for just showing up, right? I mean my physical presence means I am in the top twenty percent. For several years, I taught youth on Sunday mornings and Wednesday nights. I studied, prepared, and delivered my lessons just well enough to keep everyone happy. Their level of entertainment and interest was my measure of success, not my level of competency, ability, or preparedness.

In my professional career, I did just enough work to be better than everyone else and receive the praise that comes with it. In school, I made just good enough grades to keep my parents happy — nothing close to my full potential.

As I stood in the darkness, I realized I had never achieved my full redemptive potential in any area of my life. I had never put in the hard work or the effort needed to achieve the very best I could. As I walked back to the room, I did not speak to any of the other men. My head was down, and I was experiencing a mix of anger, regret, and personal disappointment that can come only come from a lifetime of missed opportunities.

Scaling a tree provides you a view. The quality of the view depends on the size of the tree and the scenery around it. When I scaled this tree, what I saw was myself and hated the scenery. I saw a lifelong quitter who was fooling people and doing just enough to get by.

I vowed right then that for the rest of my life, I would give my family, my employer, my church, and God my absolute best. I would pay whatever price was needed to push through the pain and discomfort and see things through to completion.

I have many dreams. I want to honor God in every area of my life. I want a lasting marriage and to raise a godly daughter. I want to impact as many pastors as possible. Some of these dreams have been realized and some are in progress. However, whatever level of progress has been made, none would have happened without a tremendous amount of hard work. General Colin Powell said, "A dream doesn't become a reality through magic; it takes sweat, determination, and hard work." I couldn't agree more.

Nick Saban added in an August 2016 ESPNU interview, "You have talent. You have to have passion, perseverance, work ethic, and discipline to be able to turn that into skill. Then have passion, perseverance, work ethic, and discipline to make that successful achievement."

Nothing great in your leadership life is ever achieved apart from hard work.

Kobe Bryant
One Apex Leader who is most associated with hard work is former Los Angeles Lakers shooting guard Kobe Bryant. After retiring from the game in 2016, his 20-year illustrious career included five NBA championships, 15 All-NBA selections, 12 All-Defensive team selections, two scoring championships, 18 All Star games, four All Star

Game MVPs, and the 2008 league MVP. Bryant finished his career with 33,643 points—the third highest total of all-time.

His work ethic is so legendary it is partially credited with dissolving his relationship with fellow superstar Shaquille O'Neil. Appearing on the September 3rd, 2015, edition of *The Lowe Post* podcast, Lakers beat writer Howard Beck said, "A lot of their differences, where they ultimately couldn't get along, had so much to do with all these other things like Kobe is maniacal about game, perfecting the game, working on his game. He's a workaholic. He's as singularly focused as anyone I've met in any walk of life. And Shaq is not."

Beck added, "Trying to squash your own impulses, your desires, your goals over and over, year after year, especially when it's because you're playing with someone who maybe doesn't treat the game as seriously as you, nobody treats the game as seriously as Kobe does."

To get a deeper sense of Bryant's work ethic and what is needed to be an Apex Leader, writer Baxter Holmes analyzed his pre-game workouts in an April 11, 2016, *ESPN.com* article.

As I read about Bryant's preparation and approach to his career, I learned what it means to work hard:

Bryant arrived to the arena four hours before tipoff to work on his craft. Hard work requires arriving early. One of the best pieces of career advice I ever received as a young man was to arrive to work 15 minutes before you are required and stay 15 minutes longer than you are scheduled. If you are willing to put in 30 extra minutes per day, you will be ahead of 80-percent of the general workforce. I immediately put this into action, and this free advice was worth more than I could ever imagine.

Hard work requires doing the lonely work. This is the work few people are willing to pay the price to do. Apex Leaders work hard when no one is looking. Only ushers and a few others were in the arena four hours before the game when Bryant took the court to practice pre-game. When questioned about this, Bryant said, "It's very peaceful. It's very quiet, and you get a chance to be in your space and in your element and hear the ball bounce, hear the sound of the net or the rim." No one is there to applaud the lonely work, but everyone applauds its results.

Hard work focuses heavily on fundamentals. Apex Leaders master the basics of their craft. Bryant began by making 15 to 20 shots with each hand, standing just below the rim. Then to work on his midrange game, he moved systematically from one baseline 15 feet from the basket to the wing. From there, he moved to the foul line and then on around the court.

He normally made 15 to 20 shots at each spot before moving on.

Hard work is necessary to get in your 10,000 hours. If you are not familiar with the The 10,000 Rule, you must read Malcolm Gladwell's classic book, *Outliers*. Gladwell theorizes that to become an expert (Apex Leader) in anything, you must put in 10,000 hours of practice prior. Bryant was an example of this. Lakers assistant coach J.J. Outlaw said, "The same moves that we see him do within the game, I can't tell you how many times he's practiced that exact same move—pump-fake, jab, pump-fake, jab, cross-over, one-dribble pull-up—in the last five years. It's been thousands of times."

What I noticed about Kobe's practice habits is hard work is done from the inside-out, not the outside-in. Most successful leaders primarily focus on what is inside them—like character and integrity—not just what people see. Bryant's shooting drills are actually a metaphor for life. Let me explain.

There is a difference between leadership development and leader development. Leadership development is developing the skills, talents, and abilities needed to accomplish a task or assignment from God. Leader development is becoming the type of man or woman who can accomplish it. Sustainable leadership is accomplished through people who work just as hard on leader development as leadership development. Failure to do so will result in a leader's talent taking her to a place where her character cannot sustain it.

We also learn several more benefits of hard work from Bryant.

Hard work helps with preparation and fast starts. You never have to recover from a good start. Because Bryant started preparing so early, he usually started fast in games.

Hard work also eliminates distractions. One of the many reasons Bryant arrived so early was so he could remain focused. He was often the only one on the floor and avoided media distractions that later-arriving players experienced.

Hard work maximizes a leader's marginal time. Life's greatest blessings are found in the margins — financial margins, emotional margins, and margins in your calendar. Apex leaders manage the margins differently than leaders who are less successful. How did Bryant manage breaks in his schedule? Instead of relaxing or shutting it down, he worked even harder. Instead of making 500 jump shots on game days, he increased it to 1,000 on off days.

Finally, hard work brings a greater sense of peace to a leader. This may sound counter intuitive, but it is true. There is a lot of chaos in a leader's life. Peace is often found through preparation. Bryant concluded, "The peacefulness of an empty arena that size is beautiful. It's a very serene experience when you're in there and there's no crowd and there's only ushers. It's a beautiful, beautiful thing." I would add that an Apex Leader who works hard is a beautiful, beautiful thing as well.

I was reminded about the sense of peace hard work can bring a leader when I visited a sandwich shop in St. Louis, Missouri. As I was waiting for my order to be filled, I read the following phrase hanging on the wall: "As a cure for worrying, hard work is better than whiskey."

Charles Woodson
Hard work also brings you great respect from others. Former Green Bay Packers and Oakland Raiders defensive back Charles Woodson is a future Hall of Famer. No one can match a resume that includes a Heisman Trophy, Defensive Rookie of the Year award, Defensive Player of the Year award, member of the 2000s All-Decade Team, and member of the Super Bowl XLV championship team. He is also the 5th all-time leading interceptor in NFL history and only player in league history with at least 50 interceptions and 20 sacks.

When told that former All-Pro Rodney Harrison

called him the greatest defensive back of all-time, Woodson told Peter King of *Monday Morning Quarterback* in a January 1st, 2016, interview, "I did see that. Man, I read it and I guess I was just kind of stuck for a minute, because that's kind of strong for someone to say that, especially an All-Pro safety, a guy who played this game for a long time, a champion. He's a defensive back himself. He's seen a lot of football, seen a lot of players, so there is a lot of validity to what he is saying because it's not just some guy. I am very humbled by that statement, but at the same time, when you work hard at something and every week you go out..." The respect from Woodson's peers caused him to then become emotional.

Hard work is vital to establishing you as a leader and giving you influence with others. A Chicago Cubs pitcher said of first baseman Anthony Rizzo in a July 19th, 2016, *Sports Illustrated* article, "I think the whole leadership thing in baseball gets overrated. What I've seen over two years is that he's a leader because he goes out and plays hard every single day. He almost never takes a day off. Never takes bats off. Believe me, he's so important to us that everybody notices that. That's leadership."

When thinking about gaining credibility as a leader, I think back to the 2013 Ohio State Buckeyes recruiting class. This group of individuals consisted of future stars Ezekiel Elliott, Joey Bosa, Eli Apple, Vonn Bell, and J.T. Barrett. They would become the core of their 2014 national championship squad. When they arrived on campus, defensive tackle Michael Bennett noted, "They like to work. They like to grind. They like to get extra lifts in. All that stuff. It's not a task for them to work hard. It's not a task for them to do another sprint. They're going to be the first guys in line. They're going to run as hard as they can, and they're going get back in the line."

The same goes for your leadership. When you put in the effort and relish the opportunity to work on your craft even more, you will move toward becoming an Apex Leader.

Tim Tebow

I have shared with you some great quotes, but my favorite speech on hard work took place on September 27th, 2008. Following a shocking one-point loss to the Ole Miss Rebels, Florida Gators Heisman Trophy winning quarterback Tim Tebow stepped up to the podium in the postgame news conference and tearfully uttered the following words:

"To the fans and everybody in Gator Nation, I'm sorry. I'm extremely sorry. We were hoping for an undefeated season. That was my goal–something Florida never has done here. I promise you one thing: a lot of good will come out of this. You will never see any player in the entire country play as hard as I will play the rest of the season. You will never see someone push the rest of the team as hard as I will push somebody the rest of the season. You will never see a team play harder than we will the rest of the season. God bless."

Following Tebow's impassioned speech, the Gators won their final eight regular season games by a total of 317 points. After defeating Alabama in the SEC Championship Game, they easily dispatched the Oklahoma Sooners 24-14 for the National Championship. Tebow's words are now immortalized in a plaque prominently displayed at the front entrance of the Florida football facility.

Hard work alone will not make you an Apex Leader, but laziness will assure you will never reach your full potential or the top of your profession. Gordon B. Hincley noted, "Without hard work, nothing grows but weeds."

But hard work alone is not enough. Let's add the next practice to the discussion—forming strong relationships.

Personal and Group Discussion Questions

1. Describe a time you suffered physically, mentally or emotionally for your success? How did you feel afterward?

2. As a leader, are you considered the hardest working person on your team? If not, what must you do to achieve this distinction, and are you willing to pay that price?

3. Name three things you are focusing the vast majority of your time and energy on. Are these activities critical to your team's success? Why?

CHAPTER 5
Apex Leaders Form Strong Relationships

The Son of Man came eating and drinking, and they say, 'Here is a glutton and a drunkard, a friend of tax collectors and sinners.'... (Matthew 11:19, NIV)

As mentioned earlier in this book, Jesus Christ is the greatest leader who ever lived. He embodies transformational leadership. One of the most impressive things about the leadership of Jesus was his continual focus on relationships.

Jesus could build a relationship with anyone. The following are just some of the people he connected with:

- The woman at the well
- Religious leaders
- Government officials
- People with disabilities
- Adulterers
- Fishermen

- Lepers
- Children
- The elderly
- Criminals
- The wealthy and the poor
- White collar and blue collar
- Men and women
- Young and old
- Healthy and sick
- Religious and irreligious people
- Emotionally healthy people
- Broken-hearted people

Through his interactions, Jesus modeled the value of people. Everything in your business depreciates—the equipment, the facilities, and the fixtures. Technology becomes outdated. Ideas have a shelf life. There is only one thing in your business which appreciates—your people, and this is where Jesus strategically spent all his time. Smart leaders do exactly the same.

The most important relationship a leader needs to cultivate and protect is the relationship with their family. This is especially true for men. This book spends a lot of time talking about other leaders–many who are very well known. But I want to take a moment and give you a picture of how forming strong relationships plays out in my home.

For many years, my favorite part of each day was coming home after work. I often finish work days with little to offer those I love the most. But after a long, hard day at the office, the following would take place:

"He's home! He's home! He's home!" For several years these words were cheered every night between 6:30 to 7:00 PM. That is when the garage door went up, my car pulled in, and I walked in the front door arriving home from a hard but productive day. It became our family tradition that when I arrived, my wife, Sonya, and daughter, Anna, would shout those six wonderful words in unison. There were hugs, kisses, and a mini-celebration. I loved my job, but I also loved coming home!

Hollywood experts tell us the initial scene of any movie is critical. The opening act sets the stage for the rest of the movie. When a man arrives home from being away, how he is welcomed sets the stage for the rest of the evening.

The level of a man's performance is in direct proportion to his wife's confidence in him. Sonya makes me feel so valued and important when I arrive home that I feel I can accomplish almost anything. Also, my family encourages me. Whatever redeemable qualities I have as a husband and father are reinforced, and their attitude compels me to become the best leader I possibly can be.

The life of a leader is joyful but also challenging—sometimes very challenging. All leaders have days they wish were simply over. When those days occur in my life, my family's loving attitude allows proper balance, perspective, and a willingness to return to work the next day. Many times at night, there are issues we have to deal with. Whether it is a phone call received earlier in the day, unwelcome mail, or the challenges of doing homework with my daughter who would rather be doing anything else, I am now able to address those items with a more positive attitude because of how Sonya helps lead our home.

There is nothing I would not do for my family. Their appreciation of my efforts simply makes me want to serve them even more and give them everything I can.

Some leaders may believe this portion of the book is completely unrealistic because their families are not cheering their arrival with, "He's home!" Know this. Great leaders will not let someone else's performance or character determine theirs.

Men, in particular, are naturally insecure. This is a big secret about men, but trust me, it is true. Men want to be heroes but are deathly afraid of failure, not measuring up, and not providing financially for those they love. This is in our DNA originating from

Adam in the Garden of Eden. When husbands are treated like the knight in shining armor they desperately want to be, more times than not, they will become one.

As a father, I also work with great diligence to strengthen my relationship with my daughter and lead her well. You may have read my dedication to her at the beginning of this book.

My leadership in Anna's life started immediately. Due to complications during childbirth, I held her for the first two hours of her life. Those poor doctors had to hear me talk to her non-stop. I told Anna how much God loved her and had a wonderful plan for her life. She was told how greatness is inherent in everyone, and she was going to make a significant impact in this world. I told her how much she was already loved by her parents and how she would grow up in a wonderful home. Little did I know what God had in store.

For the next several years, every Thursday was daddy-daughter date night while my wife attended Bible study. During this time, Anna sat on my lap and I read countless books to her. We watched television (Barney and Nickelodeon), strolled around the neighborhood or went to the park.

Saturday mornings became our weekly breakfast dates. These have become the most joy-filled memories of my life. For twelve years, Anna and I went to breakfast every Saturday morning. Panera Bread at the mall was usually our place of choice. I would talk about my week (generally held nothing back) and listen as she told me about hers. I especially enjoyed our time together because, unlike so many other relationships in my life, my daughter wanted nothing from me. She just wanted to be with me — no agenda or strings attached.

After eating our pumpkin muffins and cinnamon rolls, we would walk through the mall and go shopping wherever she liked. It became a tradition on our visits to spend a quarter on a rubber bouncing ball from the machines in the mall. If you visited my house today, I could show you multiple containers containing hundreds of rubber balls.

Each rubber ball represents a memory and an investment of time in the formation of a strong relationship. Time is one of a leader's greatest assets because once it is spent, it can never be recovered. The time I spent investing in my daughter is the greatest investment I ever made. It is something I will never regret and wish I would have invested even more.

When Anna became a teenager, I had to get far more creative in how we spent time together, but the strong foundation for our relationship was already in place.

When she graduated from high school, I wrote her the following note on behalf of her mother and I. Allow me to share it with you.

Our dearest Anna,

You accepted Jesus as your Lord and Savior at an early age and have faithfully served him with a willing heart and mind. God has had his hand on you your entire life and chosen you to do incredible things. Be strong and do it!

You have paid the price of preparation to become all God has created you to be. From the beginning, you had a plan to be a worship leader. Plans were put in place to develop your voice, your instrumental talent, your public speaking skills, and your presence on stage. Because of your hard work, practice habits, and diligence, you have excelled in all areas.

All of this comes as the result of the Lord's hand on your life.

Be strong and courageous and continue doing your work. Do not be afraid. Do not be discouraged. The Lord is with you. He will never fail you or forsake you until all his plans for your life are fulfilled. Never forget, you also have a family and vast network of pastors and church leaders who will willingly help you achieve your dreams.

You will one day become one of the world's greatest Christian leaders—male or female. Thousands will one day be influenced by your life and ministry.

Even though God has chosen you, the journey will not be easy. You have much to learn and experience. But ultimately, this is about God's glory and not your own.

Talent is never enough. Your family is committed to assist in resourcing your dreams. We have provided much and will continue doing so. You will have access to our financial resources, experience, and network of friends.

Everything is in place for you to become all God has created you to be. Are you willing to consecrate yourself before the Lord and live solely for him?

Because if you are willing to live wholeheartedly for Jesus, you will have many days of great rejoicing, and because of your life, thousands will rejoice right along with you.

Our greatest joy has been watching you grow up. But these joys will one day be surpassed as we watch you fulfill God's plan for your life and take the world by storm for his glory.

Our dearest Anna—You were born for this. You were prepared for this. You have put in the work for this. You have paid the price of preparation needed for success. And you have God to help you.

Be strong and do it!

If you want to form strong relationships notice some of the themes from my letter—pointing people to Jesus, reminding them he has a plan for their lives, investing personal resources in others, and creating a strong sense of family.

Leadership in the family is so important because you are preparing your children for the future—a future you may never see. As a husband, father and leader, I set the precedent each and every day. May I steward it well.

Now, allow me to shift gears and get a little more practical. For anyone who wants to grow in leadership and advance in an organization, here is a lesson few people will ever share:

Almost all important decisions made about you and your career take place when you are not in the room.

Think about it. When church or company leaders are meeting together and discussing who should be added to their team, you are not in the room. When resumes are being reviewed by Human Resources and it is being determined who should be interviewed, you are not in the room. When compensation packages and promotions are being discussed by executive management, you are not in the room. When staffing cuts are discussed, you are not in the room. Notice the trend.

Therefore, smart leaders are always building mutually beneficial relationships. To build strong relationships, you must treat everyone with kindness and great respect. Do not burn bridges. Always make to it a point that if someone looked at your record, every company you left, every position you held, every relationship you were involved in, you left a trail of kindness and respect. Unfortunately, many leaders leave a trail of destruction and broken relationships.

When a church is looking for a staff member, when a company is looking for an executive leader, when a sports franchise is looking for a general manager or coach, you want someone in the room to say, "Has anyone been in contact with [insert your name]? He is great. Skill, work ethic, and passion? He has it all. Let's reach out and see if he is available."

And those conversations almost always take place without you being in the room. Always leave a trail of kindness and respect behind you. To further emphasize the point, my former supervisor gave a this 26-year-old brash young man the following advice, "Brian, be careful what toes you step on.

68

They may one day be attached to the rear end you have to kiss."

The Barna Group reported in a 2009 study that senior pastors of mainline churches have an average tenure of only four years. One of the reasons cited for such a brief stay is that while 93-percent of all pastors surveyed profess to be leaders, only 12-percent claim to actually have the spiritual gift of leadership.

The epidemic of pastors leaving their churches, regardless of the reason, is an issue that must be addressed. However, since I have never been a senior pastor, I wanted someone with credibility to speak into this issue.

Dr. Brian Stowe
Dr. Brian Stowe accepted the position of Senior Pastor of Maysville Baptist Church, located in North Georgia, in 1997. In 2013, I visited their church on a couple of occasions and was immediately impressed with the love that existed between this pastor and his congregation. There was a relational connection I had experienced in only a few other places. While Brian's tenure at Maysville has since concluded, his life and leadership has been marked by the principle of building strong relationships

During the time we spent together, I felt impressed to ask Brian what he had done to allow him to have such a long tenure at this church. His answers provide a great template for all leaders.

The top reason Brian gave for his long tenure at Maysville was his "awesome wife," Bonnie. I did not expect this to be his number one answer, so I asked for further explanation. Bonnie provides him incredible support. While he was working, she kept balance between his work and home life — ensuring Brian got proper rest. Because his life was so well-balanced, she could release him during busy seasons to be at the church more often.

Building strong relationships begins with having a genuine love for people. Early in Brian's pastorate, the church experienced two tragic losses. These became milestone moments for Brian personally and also for ministry execution. He said, "You must touch people during struggles." What Brian was saying is that when those in your church are experiencing great pain or loss, you need to be intersecting their lives in a compassionate and comforting way. Conversely, Brian also made it a priority to celebrate with the church families during good times as well.

To build strong relationships with others you must first practice good self-leadership. Brian said, "It's easy to forget the power of prayer." Over 200 people had recently become Christ followers at a dinner hosted by the church. Countless round-the-clock hours of prayer went into this event. Brian noted, "God has to do it. Not us."

God gives power to a pastor's preaching. Leadership in all forms comes with a microphone. There comes a time when the leader must stand up and proclaim, "Follow me!" Brian's congregation loved hearing biblical truth and he loved preaching it. He did not give his opinion to his congregation. Brian simply preached what the Bible says. He discovered the power of simplicity. Brian pointed out that simple does not mean easy or less work. On the contrary, simple is hard work.

John Maxwell wrote in his book, *The 21 Irrefutable Laws Of Leadership*, about The Law Of The Inner Circle; "Those closest to the leader determine the success of the leader." If you want to accomplish anything great as a leader, you must surround yourself with competent staff. Brian had such a staff and commended their patience and flexibility. We laughed when he said, "Sometimes when I want to do something, they just scratch their heads and then say, 'Let's get it done.'" Brian had the further support of the church's key volunteer leaders. His deacons wanted to serve Brian and help him, and then they got out of his way and let him lead.

Because of his love for family, his love for people, his dependence upon God, and his strong inner-circle,

Brian built great trust with the congregation. In fact, he told me the story of when he was studying for his Doctorate of Ministry, and it hit him: "These people trust me." This realization moved him emotionally, and he has never done anything to break that sacred trust.

Trust is such an important element when building relationships. Brian revisited it a second time during our conversation. When he made important decisions, he communicated often with a biblical perspective always in mind. Early on, he told the congregation that the church was going to grow, reach people, and do it for the long haul. To also build trust, Brian knew you cannot leapfrog leaders. He brought them on board early, and finally, he said, "Don't do anything stupid! Don't compromise!"

Mike Linch

When it comes to being an Apex Leader in the area of forming strong relationships, few are better than Mike Linch, senior pastor of NorthStar Church in Kennesaw, Georgia. He is truly one of the kindest people I have ever met. One of his strengths is forming relationships with unchurched people who struggle with guilt from their past.

The following are some facts about people who are resistant to attending weekly services that I learned from Mike:

Unchurched people were often deeply affected as children by the actions of their parents, and this has a significant impact on their current view of God. In addition to their parents not stewarding their leadership well, those in roles of spiritual authority often judge unchurched people harshly.

Throughout their lives, they have often watched Christians treat each other harshly. Why would they want to be part of that? As a result, unchurched people think Christianity is religion and rules rather than a relationship. They have no idea how much God truly loves them.

Many unchurched people believe in God, but they have legitimate faith questions such as, "How do you gain his favor?" or "What is needed to go to heaven?" Like many people who have been a part of church, unchurched people have faced many challenges as adults and questioned God when tragedy struck.

Here is good news: Unchurched people are most likely to come to church when invited by a friend–because of relationship! They are then impressed with the excellence of the worship services even if they do not understand or believe everything being communicated. Unchurched people often do not sing during church services but enjoy messages that "demystify" the Bible.

Apex Leaders Form Strong Relationships

Unchurched people will return if they like the pastor and their children feel welcomed and loved. In fact, though they do not sing, their hearts melt when they see their children enjoying church and singing. Smart pastors and church leaders invest heavily in worship services and children's programming.

Once unchurched people become regular attenders, they will become involved in small groups and begin serving others. This provides community and strong relationships that everyone longs for.

Jesus taught a lot through his life about the importance of prioritizing relationships with unchurched people. I see Mike Linch reflecting this in his daily interactions as well. Because of how Mike loves unchurched people and forms strong relationships with them, he is truly Jesus with skin on. Mike Linch is truly an Apex Leader.

Finally, let's look at the exponential potential for good that can happen when Apex Leaders form strong relationships with other Apex Leaders. A July 5, 1991, meeting between two business titans became the catalyst for an enduring friendship which has changed the lives of hundreds of thousands of people. Interestingly, it almost never happened.

On that summer day, Microsoft CEO Bill Gates was invited to meet with Warren Buffett, the CEO and Chairman of Berkshire Hathaway, at the Gates family home. He was reluctant to do so because he thought the conversation would revolve around the buying and selling of stocks, and he did not have much interest in that sort of conversation. After all, he was too busy running Microsoft. However, Gates acquiesced when pressed to attend by his mother, Mary.

Once Gates arrived, both men immediately knew they would become close friends. They discovered they had a similar reason for their success: curiosity. Also, both were avid readers, hard workers, had positive attitudes, and had a mutual disdain for frivolous things. When Gates' father asked both men to write down the one word most responsible for their success, each wrote "focus." Gates and Buffett were kindred spirits.

In a January 29, 2017, interview at Columbia University, Buffett was asked what made his relationship with Gates so strong. Buffett gave an incredible view into the type of individuals Apex Leaders often form strong relationships with. He said, "I wanted people with similar values, similar objectives, (people who could) pour in intelligence, energy and their own funds. Every life is of equal value, (people who) see the world as I do. They want meaning and persuasive powers and getting many governments and people involved."

Apex Leaders Form Strong Relationships

The Bill and Melinda Gates Foundation is the world's largest philanthropic organization. Their desire is to bring innovation to help the world's most under-resourced individuals. As a result, 86-percent of the world's children in 2017 have access to vaccines.

In the form of Berkshire Hathaway shares, Buffett signed papers giving $31 billion of his fortune to fund the Gates Foundation's work in fighting infectious diseases and reforming education. Over time, most of his $44 billion in stock holdings will be given to the Bill and Melinda Gates Foundation.

As they witnessed the power of partnership in their own lives, Gates and Buffett invited other Apex Leaders into this process. Through an initiative called "The Giving Pledge," 156 billionaires are now pooling their resources to solve the world's most pressing issues.

These strong relationships have helped millions of people live better lives which leads us to our next practice: Apex Leaders make others better.

Personal and Group Discussion Questions

1. Take a moment and write down your thoughts about your family. Are the relationships you have within your family the most important to you? Would the members of your family say that you place a high value on your relationships with each of them? Why or Why not?

2. Jesus was a bridge builder. What types of individuals do you easily connect with? What relationships are the most difficult for you to build?

3. Write down the names of three people who, if you formed a relationship with them, would take your leadership to the next level. Now, write down a plan to connect with them.

4. As a leader, what do you think people say about you when you are not in the room? How does this make you feel?

CHAPTER 6
Apex Leaders Make Others Better

Do not be misled: "Bad company corrupts good character." (1 Corinthians 15:33, NIV)

I tell the following story only at the urging of my family. They feel it could help countless people become free from the bondage of a violent and abusive past. My family wants me to share this story in the hope that others become better rather than bitter.

The earliest memory I have of my father was when I was just five years old. My younger brother was just born and spent the first few weeks of his life in the hospital. Looking back, this undoubtedly must have caused tremendous stress on my parents. However, things reached a breaking point the day he came home from the hospital.

Imagine a standard square-sized living room. As you

enter the front door, a chair is on your immediate left and a television on your immediate right. A sofa is on the back wall, and a chair is positioned in the corner just beside the television. I was sitting in the chair on the left. Mom was sitting in the corner. My grandmother had come in to town to help with the baby. She was sitting on the sofa with dad, holding my brother.

Dad was talking to Mom about some medicine she needed to take, but Mom did not want to take it. Everything seemed normal. Mom and Dad were talking. My grandmother was holding my brother with his head resting on her shoulder.

All of a sudden, Dad jumped up off the sofa towards my mother and grabbed her by the hair on both sides of her head. With his eyes literally bulging out of his head, he stood over her and began shaking her head and screaming at her. My grandmother, still holding my baby brother, jumped and began slapping him on the back trying to get him off my mom. All the while, I am sitting in the chair taking it all in.

This is the first memory I have of my father.

The next seven years were a series of similar events: spousal abuse, physical abuse, verbal abuse, pornography, alcoholism, and adultery. These were all common in my home. Mercifully, my parents divorced in 1978.

At this point, my mother was single and had three children, twelve years old and younger. Wanting us to have some form of stability, she decided we needed to go to church. Since I was the oldest and angriest of the three, she let me choose wherever we went.

My three best friends at the time were Mark Nettles, Chuck Black, and Tim Price. Each of them attended Acworth United Methodist Church in Acworth, Georgia. I had no idea what attending a Methodist church meant or what a Christian even was. I did not know there was an Old and New Testament. I had no concept of anything spiritual. I just knew I wanted to go wherever Mark, Chuck, and Tim went.

Lenis Black
Andy Stanley says, "Following Jesus will make your life better and make you better at life." I did not know it at the time, but I desperately needed a better life. One of the people God used to help me was my high school Sunday School teacher, a man named Lenis Black. Mr. Black just happened to be Chuck's father.

I don't know where I would be today without Mr. Black. He was a great teacher who was humorous and quite interesting. Mr. Black made the Bible come alive and took a special interest in me. One event I remember in particular came several years later as I was watching the Georgetown vs. Villanova college basketball showdown in January 1984. I received an unexpected phone call from him. He had no agenda as he was calling just to check in, but it was clear to me that he was investing in my life. The funny thing is: I remember every aspect of that phone call to this very day.

The reality is that when a divorce happens, a hole is created in a child's life. It is simply unavoidable. The only winners in divorce are the lawyers. I needed an example of a godly man in my young life, and God gave me the gift of Mr. Black. He gave me a picture of what a man sold out to Jesus Christ looked like.

Because of Mr. Black and the unconditional love bestowed on me by the people of Acworth United Methodist Church, I gave my life to Jesus Christ in August 1980. Shortly thereafter, Mr. Black asked me to join him in our senior pastor's office before a morning service to pray with other church leaders for the pastor. I had no idea what was going on or even how to pray, but I went because Mr. Black was the one who asked. That is the power of influence, and that single prompting to have me in that setting propelled me on a path of serving pastors and church leaders that I am still on to this day.

Mr. Black taught our class for each of my four years of high school. Every year he wrestled with whether he should re-up for another year and return to the class. He always did, and my life was never the same.

You may work with children or young people and periodically wonder whether your investment in future generations is worth it or not. After all, they may not appear to be listening, and their growth is often incremental at best.

Using my life as a case study, I'll tell you this: you never know the impact you make when you commit to investing in others. Who knows? The person you are investing in may grow up to be someone who helps churches and writes leadership books.

No matter how talented you are, you need someone who can make you better. Shannon Sharpe was one of the greatest athletes in the NFL during the 1990's. However, he needed the help of Denver Broncos quarterback John Elway to reach his full potential.

He was quoted in the January 12, 2015, edition of *Sports Illustrated* saying, "John (Elway) told me, every play, what I was supposed to do, and he was pretty much calling his own plays. So, not only did he have to know the defense, plus change the line protection, but he'd make sure that I knew. They would put me in motion, and as I'd run past, he would turn around and tell me. I got a gold jacket because of John."

The gold jacket Sharpe refers to is the ceremonial jacket he put on when entering the National Football League Hall of Fame. John Elway made Shannon Sharpe not only a better player but helped him reach the Hall of Fame.

Walter Szulc, Jr.
To demonstrate the danger of not having people in your life who make you better, I want to discuss one of the most terrifying things anyone could experience—a shark attack. In 2012, Walter Szulc Jr. was kayaking off the beaches of Cape Cod when the dorsal fin of a great white shark appeared right behind his small craft.

Clearly visible to those watching in horror on the beach, dozens of people tried in vain to help Szulc and alert him to the impending grave danger. This horrifying moment reveals several reasons we need to accept help and allow others to speak into our lives.

Much like a shark attack, trouble often silently creeps up on you causing an instant crisis. Leaders are often completely unaware of dangers that may be lurking in their organizations. Being continually blind-sided is a luxury leaders simply cannot afford. If leaders are unaware and do not have their ears to the ground, the results could be fatal.

As discussed in the opening chapter, part of having

awareness comes from building a great team around you. Szulc was the last one to see the shark. He did not have 360-degree vision. Neither do you. A good team gives you multiple perspectives.

Pictures and eyewitness accounts showed that the shark was bigger than the kayak. When leaders wait too long to address an issue, it can reach unmanageable proportions. Once Szulc finally noticed the shark's presence, he took immediate action and paddled to shore. Passivity rarely makes a leader better. At the very least, it damages a leader's credibility.

God often uses family members to sharpen leaders' lives. Szulc's daughter told him to stay out of the water because it was too dangerous. Leaders should listen to their families. They have a sixth sense about danger and desire your best interests more than anyone else.

Szulc's daughter and the bystanders on the beach wanted to help him, but he was not listening. Not listening to wise counsel and pleas for help almost cost him his life. Not listening to others may not cost your life, but it could cost you influence.

After spotting the shark, the beaches were immediately closed by officials. However, when the lifeguards got off duty at 7:00 p.m., many swimmers re-entered the water. Sadly, there are some leaders who continually "re-enter the water" by returning to bad habits and behaviors even though they know danger is lurking. Ignoring danger places your leadership at risk.

On that day, Szulc never dreamed he would encounter a great white shark. The odds were just too small. It would never happen to him, but it did. Leaders understand that though the odds may be small, the stakes are too high to take unnecessary risks. It only takes one mistake, one miscalculation, or one error in judgment to lose all your influence.

A Special Note To Church Pastors
Other than my family, the people I listen to the most are pastors and church staff. Not only have they always wanted my personal best interests, but I have also found they want your best interests as well.

Many of you reading this book may be a pastor or a church staff member. If so, I want to say something directly to you. I believe you have the most difficult job in the world. While it has unbelievable highs and on its best days is the most rewarding occupation/calling in the world, it is also the most difficult.

You have given your lives to serve people. As a result, the two most important words I, and everyone else under your leadership, can ever say is "THANK YOU."

Thank you for going to God on our behalf and praying for us daily. Thank you for studying God's Word and communicating biblical truths in such a compelling fashion.

I want to thank your family for their generosity. Specifically, I appreciate their willingness to live in a fishbowl and for sharing you with us. Many of you cannot even take your family to a restaurant or movie without being disturbed by a "well-meaning" church member. I also want to thank you for modeling generosity and never allowing us to pick up a lunch tab.

While some may have had negative church experiences, that is not reflective of my experience. I want to thank you for demonstrating grace, love, and patience when people have questioned your motives and competency. Sheep may be dumb, but they bite and have a particular taste for pastors and church staff.

You likely did not go into ministry to become wealthy. Thank you for paying the price of preparation by getting such a great education and then taking a compensation package well below the level of your education.

Pastoring is incredibly hard work. Thank you for putting in countless hours and for being humble enough to be a continual learner. Thank you for being men and women of impeccable character and integrity. Thank you for the courage to make hard decisions and then live with the results.

Thank you for seeing what we could be through the power of Jesus Christ and not just what we currently are. Thank you for helping us discover and use our spiritual gifts, allowing us to live lives of meaning and purpose.

Thank you for having the courage to tell us about the sin in our lives and our need for repentance and a Savior. Thank you for expanding and helping shape our biblical worldview. Thank you for creating environments which help us raise Godly children.

Thank you for presiding over the landmark moments in our lives–baptisms, weddings, and funerals. When a landmark moment happens, a pastor is almost always there.

Life is hard. Thank you for walking with us through tragedy, marital troubles, raising children, and life's great challenges. Thank you for the periodic phone calls, texts, and emails just to see how we are doing.

Thank you for your great faith in what God can do. Our faith increases by watching you. We draw inspiration and strength from your life.

And most of all, thank you for not quitting each

Monday.

Also, please forgive us for not being better friends. Being a pastor is the loneliest job in the world. We should have been there for you and your family more often. Forgive us for not paying you more money and not praying for you more often. We are sorry for not being as passionate as we could be about the church's mission and vision. And how we wish we would have brought more of our unchurched friends to weekend services.

Much like Mr. Black, we will thank you every day, for all of eternity, for serving the church and our Lord so well. "Thank You" is not nearly enough, but I hope these two words encourage you today. Pastor, no profession makes people better than you.

Times of Crisis
Apex Leaders who make others better are most needed during times of crisis. In 2006, Hurricane Katrina devastated the Gulf Coast region causing an estimated $160 billion in damage. The hardest area hit was the city of New Orleans. More than 800,000 homes were damaged or destroyed during the storm. Tragically, 1,833 individuals perished.

It was shortly thereafter that Drew Brees was signed as quarterback of the New Orleans Saints.

After being released by the San Diego Chargers

because of a shoulder injury, the Saints were the only team to offer Brees a contract. Few players wanted to come to New Orleans. The city was a ghost town. Homes were destroyed. Schools for the players' children were woefully damaged. The quality of life away from the field was well-below that of other NFL cities. Something as simple as going to a drug store was a challenge. Brees admitted in an August 28, 2015, *CNN Money* article, "A lot of guys came here in 2006, including myself, as somewhat of castaways. Many of us did not have many other options."

Led by Brees and head coach Sean Payton, the team became a symbol of hope for this city and gave the residents something to be excited about. Brees observed, "As people are trying to rebuild their homes, rebuild their lives, they're still coming to games to cheer on the Saints because it just gives them so much energy and enthusiasm…just this feeling that we're all in this together."

The journey back for both Brees personally and the city of New Orleans was cemented with the team's 2010 Super Bowl victory. Brees said, "When we won that Super Bowl, it was that culmination of all those ups and downs, all those hardships. [It was] just that sheer elation of, we've done it, and we've done it together."

Brees' service to the city is not limited to the football field. In 2003, he and his wife, Brittany, started the Brees Dream Foundation to help cancer patients and provide care, hope, education, and opportunities for those in need. As part of helping with the hurricane recovery efforts, Brees formed a partnership with Operation Kids in 2007. Together, they began rebuilding the city's parks, athletic facilities, and playgrounds, and they launched mentoring programs in the local schools. Brees and the city of New Orleans will forever be linked.

Ralph Waldo Emerson said, "It is one of the true compensations of this life that a man can not help another without also helping himself." Emerson would have liked Drew Brees.

Personal and Group Discussion Questions

1. Andy Stanley says, "Following Jesus will make your life better and make you better at life." As a leader, how has following Jesus made your life better?

2. List three things a teacher, coach, family member, pastor, or mentor did to make a positive difference in your life.

3. How are you currently investing in the lives of others? Be specific.

CHAPTER 7

Apex Leaders Show Consistency

"...Daniel, servant of the living God, has your God, whom you serve continually, been able to rescue you from the lions?" (Daniel 6:20, NIV)

Few individuals in the Old Testament modeled consistency better than Daniel. As a young Hebrew man who found himself in Babylonian captivity, Daniel provides a timeless example of how consistent private integrity results in public influence.

The stories of Daniel are legendary, but no story can match his imprisonment in the den of lions. Fellow government officials, who were jealous of Daniel, hatched a plot against him. They wanted to have Daniel killed and removed from his position of influence, but instead of a horrific ending, we are given the ultimate lesson of consistency when leading during times of crisis.

Daniel lived a life of integrity. He likely had few regrets. Let those words sink in for a moment: A life of integrity without regrets. Think about it. Can you say the same thing? If not, take the necessary steps to make your situation right.

Daniel 6:4 shares, "So the governors and satraps sought to find some charge against Daniel concerning the kingdom; but they could find no charge or fault, because he was faithful; nor was there any error or fault found in him." In modern terms, Daniel would be described as a boy scout. The lesson here is that consistent, faithful living allows you to be above reproach. This kind of living creates leadership that is full of character and integrity.

Daniel 6:10 tells us, "And in his upper room, with his windows open toward Jerusalem, he knelt down on his knees three times that day, and prayed and gave thanks before his God, as was his custom since early days." Why was Daniel such a trusted and respected leader? It was not because of the things he did publicly. Daniel was an effective public leader because it was his custom to pray three times a day privately.

As a leader, your ability to handle conflict, crisis, disappointments, shifts in the market, downturns in the economy, false accusations, and challenging times is often not determined by your competence.

Rather, your ability to lead at a high level is predetermined by how well you lead yourself when no one is looking. Daniel could withstand the plot against him, imprisonment, and the death sentence of being held captive with hungry lions because of his consistent, private prayer life.

A blameless and faithful life gives you influence and favor with even the most powerful leaders. When David was being imprisoned, King Darius said, "May your God, whom you serve continually, deliver you." Faithful, dependable, and consistent lives are rare. Leaders of this sort are invaluable to organizations.

God honors leaders who consistently live to honor him. Even if you work for someone who is not a Christian, history shows that oftentimes they will look at you and say, "I don't necessarily believe what you do, but you are so faithful, so dependable, so hard-working, so trustworthy, so committed to our organization, and so consistently helpful, I wish I had a 100 more like you."

This is the power of consistent leadership.

To say Jesus was consistent would be a gross understatement. He never wavered. In fact, the writer of Hebrews said, "Jesus Christ the same yesterday, and today, and forever." Similarly, Apex Leaders are consistent. They are reliable. You can set your watch by them. Because of their consistency, they bring peace and security to those in your organization.

Willow Creek Community Church located in South Barrington, Illinois, created a set of core values that have become axioms for many of today's Christian communities. One of the values is: "Excellence honors God and inspires people."

While this value has proven to be true, sadly, I have noticed that consistent excellence becomes viewed as "average" in the eyes of others when they are surrounded by the best. In other words, because of a lack of perspective, a sense of entitlement, or just plain boredom, some leaders lack an appropriate amount of appreciation for the excellence they experience daily.

This is why men leave their beautiful wives for cheap thrills or counterfeit relationships. This is why congregations find fault with incredible pastors. This is why bored leaders randomly fire top employees in hopes of finding someone "to take them to the next level." In each of these instances, the organizations and their people suffer because of a lack of appreciation for consistent excellence.

Mark Richt
One such event took place on November 29, 2015. It was on this date the University of Georgia Bulldogs

and Mark Richt mutually agreed to end his tenure as the school's head football coach. This move is representative of all that is wrong in college sports specifically, and our nation as a whole. His removal shows a complete lack of understanding of what it means to be a successful leader.

Coach Richt, a two-time SEC champion, had many notable accomplishments prior to his departure. He is one of only seven head coaches in NCAA history to have 90 wins in his first nine seasons. Coach Richt coached 64 players who were drafted by the NFL during his 11 years — the most during that time among all teams in the highly competitive SEC.

During his 15 years at Georgia, Coach Richt amassed a 144-51 regular season record along with a 9-5 bowl record. He was the SEC East champion on five separate occasions.

Coach Richt was only one year removed from his sixth Top 10 finish and had nine wins in 2015 with a chance to make it ten at the bowl game.

What many will remember about the Mark Richt era is the lasting impact of his Christian leadership. Other than the man who led him to Christ in 1986, former Florida State head coach Bobby Bowden, I have never witnessed a coach who represented Jesus Christ in such an honorable fashion. Proof was provided when Richt was honored with the 2013

Stallings Award for commitment to humanitarian and community service.

Of all his student athletes, 222 graduated with a degree — the most in the SEC during his tenure. Coach Richt is proof that consistent excellence becomes average when it is all you have.

Mark Richt was unemployed for all of three days when his alma mater, the University of Miami, announced he was hired to be the new football coach.

Jack Arthur
Another leader who demonstrated consistent excellence was Jack Arthur. Jack and his wife Kay lead Precept Ministries, a worldwide ministry dedicated to the inductive study of God's Word. They had a burning passion to see people meet God in the Scriptures and learn to study the Bible for themselves. This ministry has been an incredible blessing to multiple generations of my family.

On one particular visit to their campus in Chattanooga, Tennessee, my daughter and I were walking alongside a creek located on their property. I showed her the exact spot where her mother and I sat down and asked God what level of financial support we should give to the ministry. Then I told her I wrote the largest check I have written to date, and I could not have been happier. It was a wonderful time to make a lasting impact in her life in the area of generosity. We then walked back into the main facility and waited to meet my wife. Then a wonderful surprise took place.

Jack Arthur himself walked up and began talking to us! I often start each day by asking God to "wonderfully surprise me today," but the 30 minutes with this spiritual giant were something truly special.

At the time, Jack was in his eighties and had made an impact with his life like few others. He told us stories about being a missionary in Nigeria, killing cobras, encountering pythons, his family, and the history of Precept Ministries.

One of my favorite stories he told was when Precept almost ceased to exist. Precept had enough financial resources to last through the end of a month. The leadership had asked God to intervene, and if he did not, then they would all go into the parking lot, hold hands, sing a praise song, and collectively ask what he had for them to do next.

Because their ministry is located on a farm, they owned several horses. As the end of the month was approaching, a storm came through causing lightning to strike and kill a horse. The insurance money from the horse's death allowed them to continue operations, and the rest is history. During the recession of 2008, they were one of the few 501(c)(3) ministries operating in the black.

Jack was an incredible man, and the impact of his leadership will be felt for eternity. He truly was an Apex Leader. The main compliment I can give him is this: I think he loved Jesus more than anyone I have ever met. The leadership principles we all can take from his life are the following:

Jack Arthur had a clear, consistent, single focus — the Word of God. He had a HUGE vision with a ministry that still has worldwide impact.

Jack also consistently modeled generosity. He honored those who made the Precept operation possible by going out of his way to say "Thank You." And most importantly, Jack loved people by generously giving of his time.

On January 9, 2017, Jack passed away peacefully with his wife of 51 years by his side. What Jack knew by faith, he then knew by sight. He went home to be with Jesus. I hope my daughter will one day understand what a privilege it was for her to meet him: a godly leader who lived a lifetime of consistent excellence.

No athlete ever demonstrated consistent excellence better than the legendary Hank Aaron. Aaron is still considered by many as the all-time professional baseball home run champion with 755 roundtrippers. What is interesting about his achievement is he never hit more than 47 home runs in a single season.

Apex Leaders Show Consistency

From 1955 through 1974, he hit between 20 and 47 home runs each season. For the greatest home run hitter ever, there was never a 50, 60 or 70 home run season. Aaron just delivered remarkably consistent excellence. Here are his home run numbers during that 20-year stretch: 27-26-44-30-39-40-34-45-44-24-32-44-39-29-44-38-47-34-40-20.

We over-celebrate big results and under-appreciate consistent excellence. Aaron reminds us greatness is not always achieved through short-term spectacular results but sometimes through long-term consistency.

Apex Leaders consistently communicate their organization's vision. They must paint a picture of a preferred future and invite people to join them on the journey. Every leader at some point has to proclaim, "This is where we are going! Follow me!"

But vision has an innate problem. It is fueled by passion, and passion leaks. The vision does not leak, but the passion for the vision always leaks. Life's pressures are often the enemy of a compelling vision. They can drown it out. The passion for the vision must be continually refueled.

Knowing this, leaders must consistently proclaim the vision over and over and over again. You cannot share the vision enough. As Andy Stanley often reminds us: just when you are getting sick of sharing the vision is when everyone else is starting to get it.

Nothing great happens in a leader's life without consistency. When coaching leaders, I advise them to develop consistency in the following areas:

Personal Growth Leaders should be continual learners. You should always be reading, listening to podcasts, experiencing new things, and having your assumptions challenged.

Financial Responsibility Proverbs 21:5 (NIV) says, "The plans of the diligent lead to profit as surely as haste leads to poverty." Leaders should be saving, planning for the future, and living on a budget.

Humility Leaders should think of themselves less and continually point out how God is using other people and then work to help expand those other leader's platforms.

Coaching Everyone gets better with a coach. If you are looking for personal coaching, pay for someone who can help you get better in one specific area of your career or life.

Individual Character Always watch your character. If not, your talent will take you to a place your character cannot sustain you.

Communication Skills Leadership comes with a

microphone. Smart leaders are always looking for ways to improve their ability to communicate and connect others to their organization's mission and vision.

Physical Health This is the one which, if neglected, takes many leaders down. Sadly, you often cannot recover from serious health issues, and this limits your availability.

Accountability Iron sharpens iron. Leaders always get better when they are transparent with wise and trusted friends who have their best interests in mind.

Family The greatest and most important leadership takes place at home. When you have attended your final meeting, preached your final message, or played in your final game, it is your family who will be there when you go home. They deserve a greater investment of your time and energy than your career does.

Time with God The senior pastor of Transformation Church, Derwin Gray, who was also a former NFL player, once told me, "The NFL taught me everything about conditional love. Jesus Christ taught me everything about unconditional love." I agree with Derwin. My experience is that most people's love for me is based upon what I can deliver. Jesus Christ loves us just because that is who he is.

Being consistent in these areas of your life will often result in increased influence and public platforms. Platforms for Christian leaders can prove to be an interesting thing. At any given time there are about two-dozen pastors on the standard conference speaking circuit. We all know who they are. I have had the privilege of becoming friends with many. They absolutely love Jesus, their families, their churches, and want to invest deeply in other leaders. They are worthy stewards of the platform that God, through his grace, has provided them.

Dr. Crawford Loritts is one of those conference regulars. He has taught me that most of the leaders on the conference speaking circuit did not seek out those opportunities. One of his personal axioms is: Faithfulness and consistency are the platforms for greatness.

He mentors many young pastors and teaches them not to focus on personal platforms, but rather to focus on consistency and faithfulness. Dr. Loritts advises leaders to never seek out public platforms. If it is God's plan for your life, allow him to bring you those opportunities. He concludes by noting that because your focus has always been on private consistency and faithfulness this will then sustain your public platform.

Therefore, continue your daily consistency and

faithfulness. Stay humble. If, in his goodness, God gives you a national platform, take comfort in knowing you did not seek it out. You were summoned by God, and he has prepared you for the assignment.

Nowhere in the Bible did God call anyone to an easy task. Becoming an Apex Leader is hard, but I would encourage you to stop, look around and take great joy in the incredible work God has allowed you to do. Most likely you have exercised consistent and faithful leadership to get where you are, but do not discount the faithfulness and consistency of God as well. Many times we are inconsistent in our leadership, and it is only by the grace of God anyone becomes an Apex Leader.

If you are experiencing unhealthy ambition, envy, jealousy, self-imposed pressure, and anger and have hurt others as a result, please take a moment to make it right. Close this book, pick up your phone, and make the difficult call to begin healing those relationships.

It is the broken, humble, consistent, and faithful leader God uses the most.

Personal and Group Discussion Questions

1. What are some daily disciplines you already practice as a leader? What are some you wish to develop?

2. Describe three things your closest team members are doing with consistent excellence. Now, do the same for each of your immediate family members.

3. Is your love for Jesus Christ and others growing each day or shrinking? Why?

CHAPTER 8

Apex Leaders Give Generously

Now, brethren, we wish to make known to you the grace of God which has been given in the churches of Macedonia that in a great ordeal of affliction their abundance of joy and their deep poverty overflowed in the wealth of their liberality. (2 Corinthians 8:1-2, NASB)

I struggle with most modern definitions of Christian generosity. Unfortunately, I feel the word "generosity" has been hijacked. Generosity is obviously a biblical term, but I often hear pastors say, "I don't want to talk about tithing. I want to develop a culture and lifestyle of generosity." The concern I have is that all forms of accountability are removed when generosity is used in this way. In fact, speaking in these terms puts people in the place of God to determine what level of financial or lifestyle commitment equals generosity.

For instance, if I have my pastor in the car with me and we go through a drive-thru at my local Chick-Fil-A, and I purchase the lunch for the car behind me, I am classified as "generous." Even though I am robbing God of giving tithes and offerings, some may view me as a generous person.

Many pastors enjoy preaching on generosity as well. It is an easier message to preach than responsibility giving or the tithe. In fact, pastors are now even encouraged to talk about generosity rather than tithing. This is because those who give responsibly are at embarrassingly low numbers. *Relevant* magazine reported in a May 8, 2016, article that only 5-percent of professing Christians tithe. Furthermore, Christians give only 2.5-percent per capita compared to 3.3-percent during the Great Depression. Let's be honest, why make 98-percent of your church angry?

For those in the audience, generosity is also an easier message to hear because, once again, they are left with no measurable form of behavior. They are not called into any form of accountability or standard.

The pastor is happy because everyone said, "Good sermon, pastor." The congregation is happy because they were made to feel good because cooking their neighbor a meal got them off the hook from a financial commitment. Everyone wins except the lives of the poor, under-resourced, diseased, orphaned, widowed, and spiritually lost who would have been the beneficiaries of an estimated $165 billion of Kingdom revenue if all Bible-believing, blood-washed Christ-followers tithed. But at least the person behind me got a free lunch and the passenger in my car called me "generous."

God is calling leaders to more than just generosity. Generosity (as defined here) is not enough. He is calling leaders to sacrifice. The following is an easy formula to remember:

Responsibility (Tithe) + Generosity = Sacrifice. It is sacrifice that God wants.

Even though we may have misappropriated the word, God is calling us to generosity. So, what are the practices of a generous lifestyle? One of the best pictures of generosity recorded in all of Scripture is King David just prior to his death. 1 Chronicles 28 and 29 gives a detailed account of King David transitioning the kingdom to his son Solomon. What strikes me about King David's generosity is it goes beyond just being a financial act to help fund the construction of the Temple. In addition to his financial support, he also provided a true picture of what a generous life looks like.

King David invested in Solomon spiritually. He discipled him. In I Chronicles 28:9, David taught Solomon about the importance of knowing, serving, and seeking God.

King David was generous with his praise and encouragement. On multiple occasions he reminded Solomon he was selected by God and should be strong and do the work he was called to. Leaders know encouragement is never enough. You also need a plan to be successful. Knowing he would not be alive to see it, King David generously gave Solomon all the plans he had previously made for the Temple's construction.

Regarding being generous with his personal finances, King David made an estimated $4+ billion investment in today's money for the Temple's construction.

King David was also generous with his platform and influence. He praised Solomon in front of the entire Jewish nation. The lesson here for all leaders is that a personal platform is not just for personal benefit or gain. Leaders should always use their influence and platform for shining the spotlight on others and improving the lives of as many people as possible.

Finally, King David was generous in the area of pure joy. He celebrated accomplishment. A leader who does not celebrate is a leader not worth following. It was written that King David "rejoiced" when the people gave willingly, and the Temple was funded. King David demonstrated that a leader's success and true joy is found in the success of others.

The model of a generous life is investing in spiritual truth, intellectual capital, money, praise, encouragement, influence, and joy in other people's lives.

When Jesus Christ intersects an Apex Leader's life, generosity is the natural response. Upon meeting Jesus, Zacchaeus' first response was to give his wealth away. If you have financial leaders in your church not living a generous lifestyle, they may not have had a transformational encounter with the most generous leader ever. As a generous leader, what comes to you must, and will, flow through you.

Dr. Johnny Hunt, the incomparable senior pastor of First Baptist Church in Woodstock, Georgia, says, "I've never missed anything I've given away."

Speaking of financial leaders, I am fascinated by how they think, approach life, and make decisions. After studying their behaviors for over a decade, I want to share what I have found so pastors can better disciple their financial leaders.

It may sound counter-intuitive, but financial leaders are often very lonely. They are not alone–just often lonely. Everyone wants something from them and requests are frequently made for their money. Requests come from employees wanting raises, extended family members, people wanting them to invest in their ideas, alma maters, local nonprofits, and do not ever forget about their children. They do not know who they can really trust and deeply long for authentic relationships.

My experience with financial leaders is once relationships are built, they become extraordinarily generous. They remember the sacrifices they made early in life and want to make a significant difference in the lives of others. Financial leaders think big-picture thoughts and want to see how their efforts help make a larger vision become reality. They want to be part of a story bigger than themselves.

Do not under-challenge or avoid financial leaders in your life. They take their responsibilities seriously. Give them tasks worthy of their involvement. A great vision attracts financial leaders. A small vision repels financial leaders. These leaders also care about their legacy. They want to accomplish something great with their lives and are intentional about doing so.

Financial leaders are risk-takers by nature and unafraid of failure. However, do your homework. Financial leaders deal in reality–not fantasy. Commitment will be low if they feel projects or initiatives are poorly planned and unachievable.

Finally, financial leaders understand return on investment. Matthew 6:21 shares, "For where your

111

treasure is, there your heart will be also." Pastors, no one has more treasure in your ministry than your financial leaders. The Scripture would then teach no one has more heart in your ministry. No one is rooting for you more than your financial leaders. No one is hoping you succeed more. They are deeply committed to the ministry's success and have put their money where their heart is.

I mentioned that financial leaders are often lonely and looking for authentic relationships. This gives pastors a unique opportunity because they can have the one relationship with financial leaders no one else can have. They can be their pastor.

Pastors, when you meet with financial leaders, do not talk only about money. Talk about the condition of their soul. Are they saved? How is their family? How are their children doing? What does their work/life balance look like? What are they struggling with? What can you pray with them about?

Also, never ask financial leaders to come to your office. Go to them. Visit their plant or place of business. Walk around their facility and hear their story. Allow them to introduce you to their employees. If you value what financial leaders value, they will then value what you value.

Generosity is nothing new. There was once a time

described in Acts 2:45 when people in local churches sold their goods and possessions to help anyone in need. That level of generosity seems so extravagant that it could never happen in today's society, right?

Kevin Cross

Thanks to Fellowship Bible Church in Roswell, Georgia, I saw the book of Acts come to life in the fall of 2011. With many of its members still reeling from the devastation of the 2008 recession, the church conducted a "Give Til It Helps" generosity initiative. Some would call it a capital campaign. Similar to the early church, all the campaign's proceeds would go to anyone in the church who was in need.

The story of what God did during the next year was so compelling, CBS National News aired a feature on the church's generosity initiative and its stewardship pastor, Kevin Cross, during its Tuesday, May 8th, 2012, telecast.

As I watched the feature, I was amazed at the skill, work ethic, passion, and giftedness of Kevin. He showcased the leadership skills needed to be an effective stewardship pastor.

As a stewardship pastor and licensed certified public accountant, Kevin equips families, both in one-on-one and large group settings, with the tools needed to win with their finances. He also heads a panel of four highly capable individuals who, during the

"Give Til It Helps" initiative, oversaw the distribution of the funds. His role protects the church from those with bad intentions and provides accountability in the process.

Kevin's ability to help create a culture of generosity has resulted in countless people finding jobs, reliable transportation and affordable housing. Sadly, many people still reject his advice and continue the cycle of poor financial decisions and even poverty.

He would tell you that a generous spirit is often birthed out of pain. Kevin's past includes embezzlement and incarceration. However, his life was changed forever when he met Jesus while in prison. As he often says, "I used to love money and use people. Now I love people and use money."

The news feature also taught us that generosity actually begins at home. Kevin is married with two children. He is first and foremost a child of God. Second, he is an amazing husband and father. Fellowship's senior pastor, Crawford Loritts, often says, "As fathers, each day we set a precedent and send people forth into a time they cannot see." Kevin is leaving a legacy of generosity.

CBS News came to our church looking for a compelling story but found so much more. What they found was Kevin. More specifically, what they found was God using Kevin to impact the lives of others through his generosity.

When it comes to leaving a legacy of generosity, few can compare to the legendary former head basketball coach of the University of North Carolina Tar Heels, Dean Smith. One month after his 2015 death, Coach Smith provided a parting financial gift to each of the 180 letterman who played for him during his 36-year tenure.

I know what leaving a legacy of generosity meant to his players. Last impressions last. Let me explain:

Earlier in this book, I mentioned my parents. In a single year both passed away. My dad likely died without Jesus Christ in his life, but at his funeral, I helped organize a memorial service that would have honored the finest pastor. However, he left my family nothing in his will.

When my mother passed, just like Coach Smith had done for his players, she left me a financial gift. The amount of money did not matter. It was a demonstration of where her heart was.

I honored my father in his death. Because of her generosity, my mother honored me in hers.

I want to leave you with these final words regarding generosity: *"A good man leaveth an inheritance to his children's children ..."* Proverbs 13:22 (KJV).

Personal and Group Discussion Questions

1. How would you define generosity? As a leader, are you growing or shrinking in generosity?

2. How do you define sacrifice?

3. What are some things you are willing to sacrifice in your life? What are some things that are off-limits?

4. Proverbs 13:22 says, "A good man leaves an inheritance to his children's children." Have you created a will to protect your loved ones when your time on Earth is done? If not, take immediate steps to do so today.

CHAPTER 9
Apex Leaders Lead By Example

Don't let anyone look down on you because you are young, but set an example for the believers in speech, in conduct, in love, in faith and in purity. (1 Timothy 4:12, NIV)

One of the most analyzed books in the Bible concerning leadership principles is Nehemiah. Nehemiah is one of the greatest leaders in Scripture and his leadership during the rebuilding of the walls around Jerusalem has provided a template for many modern-day people of influence.

Nehemiah displayed many skills including: project management, organization, vision casting, and team building. However, what I enjoy most concerning this great leader was his ability to lead by example.

While many previous government officials took advantage of its citizens by overworking and overtaxing them, Nehemiah stayed faithful to the people and his God-given assignment by personally working on the wall. In fact, all of his servants worked right alongside of him.

Because his people were in bondage, Nehemiah refused to partake in all the trappings of success. He led by example by denying himself the finest food and drink.

When the people saw Nehemiah denying himself and standing at the wall with his servants, it inspired his countrymen to follow suit.

In the epic movie, *Passion Of The Christ*, there is a poignant scene when Jesus is standing by when Pontius Pilate reaches into a basin of water and washes his hands. At this moment, Jesus reflects on a time when he had reached into another basin of water and washed the feet of his disciples. Two leaders — one served himself by washing his own hands. The other served others by washing their feet.

All leaders fall into one of two categories — they serve themselves (hands) or they serve others (feet). Be someone who leads by example in serving others. You want to be a picture of the desired destination at which others should wish to arrive.

Great leaders, transcendent leaders, memorable leaders, lead by example.

J.D. Greear

One such leader is J.D. Greear, the senior pastor of The Summit Church in Raleigh-Durham, North Carolina, and author of such great books as *Gaining By Losing: Why the Future Belongs to Churches That Send* and *Gospel: Recovering the Power That Made Christianity*. Approximately 10,000 people attend The Summit Church's weekend services.

On June 16, 2016, few, if any, were talking about the size and scope of Greear's ministry or the many books he had written. They were talking about his class, honor, generosity, and selflessness.

For example, Mark Marshall, senior pastor of The Glade Church in Mount Juliet, Tennessee, tweeted: "The move just made by @jdgreear to concede is the classiest I've seen in 20+ SBC conventions I've attended!" What move was Mark referring to?

J.D. and Senior Pastor Steve Gaines of Bellevue Baptist Church in Memphis, Tennessee, were the two final candidates in the running for the Southern Baptist Convention presidency. America's largest denomination was facing a divided constituency. Gaines represented the old guard. He was the establishment candidate. Greear represented a new generation of younger, out-of-the-box thinkers. In fact, the name of his church does not even include the word "Baptist." The convention seemed split right down the middle by generational lines.

Heading into a too-close-to-call run-off vote, Greear chose to lead by example. He unexpectedly removed his name from consideration and conceded the election to Gaines. His actions taught several things about leading by example.

You cannot lead by example if you do not effectively lead yourself first. The best way to do this is through prayer. This is why Greear's words, "I spent a good amount of time last night praying," resonate with me so much. I need God's intervention in my life as a leader. The task he has called you and I to is too important to face alone.

Leading by example means putting the mission of your organization above your personal aspirations. Greear put the mission of the convention ahead of his desire for presidency. A leader worth following is one who makes great sacrifices for the good of others. It is counter-intuitive, but Greear's decision to remove himself from the positional leadership role of convention president actually increased his influence with the convention.

Leaders who lead by example fight for unity. Greear knew the attendees needed to leave the city of St. Louis unified. As a result, the two candidates, who represented minor points of difference with the constituents, needed a sense of resolution. Leading by example means building bridges, breaking down walls, making phone calls, walking across rooms, extending a friendly hand, and being willing to back down. Leading by example requires a sense of resolve and courage very few have.

Greear reminds us that leading by example means focusing on what is most important. He said, "We are united by a gospel too great and a mission too urgent to let any lesser thing stand in our way…one of the candidates leaving the convention with a 51 to 49 victory on a third ballot is just not going to serve our mission well." When you focus on what is most important, momentum, people, and resources flow your way. This type of leadership is magnetic. It attracts things.

At the conclusion of Greear's announcement, the audience showed their appreciation with a prolonged standing ovation. His speech was also the defining moment of the convention. This is what happens when you lead by example.

A denominational leader walked up to me afterwards and said, "Wow! Well played." Oftentimes, all people talk about at mainline denominational gatherings are things that have brought a certain level of embarrassment or discord. Greear's act was an example of everything good about Christian leadership.

Because of how he led by example, Greear is nearly certain to be elected as the next Convention president at the conclusion of Gaines' tenure. Leaders who lead by example are always honored and eventually elevated.

Pat Summitt

Few Apex Leaders have ever led by example and cleared the path for others better than the late Pat Summitt, head basketball coach for the University of Tennessee Lady Volunteers.

As we reflect on her life and career, allow me to make the case for Coach Summitt being the greatest collegiate coach of any sport in history.

In addition to coaching the 1984 Women's Olympic gold medal team, her Lady Volunteers won eight NCAA championships. Coach Summitt was the first coach in college basketball, men's or women's, to amass 1,000 victories. In fact, she finished with a 1,098–208 record. Her career winning percentage was an astounding 84.1 percent! She never had a losing season in 38 years as a head coach.

While the victories are impressive by anyone's standards, what impresses me most is the impact the seven-time National Coach of the Year had on people. Because of the example she set, 18 of her assistant coaches became head coaches. What is even more incredible is EVERY player she ever coached graduated. That's right. As a coach, she had a 100-percent graduation rate.

Unlike Bear Bryant, John Wooden, and Nick Saban, Coach Summitt was there at her sport's infancy. Women's college basketball was largely built on her hard work and commitment.

Pat Summitt was named head coach of the Lady Vols in 1974 as a 22-year-old. At that time, women's college basketball was not even recognized as a Division I sport. Coach Summitt had to purchase the team's uniforms through doughnut sales and then wash those uniforms herself.

Summitt once told *Time* magazine in a February 2009 interview, "I had to drive the van when I first started coaching. One time, for a road game, we actually slept in the other team's gym the night before. We had mats. We had our little sleeping bags."

No other person in the pantheon of great college head coaches ever had to do such tasks as a head coach. Once again, there was no D-1 Women's Basketball prior to her arrival.

Longtime rival UConn head coach, Geno Auriemma, summed it up by telling *USA Today* in its July 8, 2016, edition, "One would be hard-pressed to name a figure who had a more indelible impact on her profession than Pat Summitt. Pat set the standard for which programs like ours dreamed of achieving, both on and off the court. Our sport reached new heights thanks to her success." In 2012, Coach Summit was rightfully honored with the Presidential Medal of Freedom.

Coach Summit's father told her after her very first loss, "You don't take donkeys to the Kentucky Derby. You better get you some race horses." In essence, Coach Summitt ultimately wound up taking an entire sport to the Kentucky Derby.

Jesus Christ
Of all the leaders whose example you would want to follow, none can compare with Jesus Christ. Do you want to lead like Jesus? Who wouldn't? Jesus is the greatest leader who ever lived. I love studying Jesus and the things he did during his earthly ministry.

One of the Bible's most famous historical events was when Jesus walked on the water, found in Matthew 14:22-33. As I read the text from a leadership perspective, I discovered 13 leadership lessons we can learn from Jesus.

Apex Leaders provide clear directions for their team. Verse 22: "Immediately Jesus made the disciples get into the boat and go on ahead of him to the other side, while he dismissed the crowd."

Apex Leaders schedule times of solitude. Verse 23:

"After he had dismissed them, he went up on a mountainside by himself to pray. Later that night, he was there alone,"

Apex Leaders identify challenges. Verse 24: "and the boat was already a considerable distance from land, buffeted by the waves because the wind was against it."

Apex Leaders engage these challenges. Verse 25: "Shortly before dawn Jesus went out to them, walking on the lake."

Apex Leaders do what only they can do in an organization. Verse 26: "When the disciples saw him walking on the lake …"

Apex Leaders listen to their teams. Verse 26: "they were terrified. 'It's a ghost,' they said, and cried out in fear."

Apex Leaders immediately respond to their teams' concerns. They are not passive. Verse 27: "But Jesus immediately said to them: 'Take courage! It is I. Don't be afraid.'"

Apex Leaders are clear communicators. Verses 28 and 29: "'Lord, if it's you,' Peter replied, 'tell me to come to you on the water.' 'Come,' he said."

Apex Leaders give their teams permission to fail. Verse 30: "But when he saw the wind, he was afraid and, beginning to sink,"

Apex Leaders provide solutions. Verse 31: "Immediately Jesus reached out his hand and caught him."

Apex Leaders look for teachable moments. Verse 31: "'You of little faith,' he said, 'why did you doubt?'"

Apex Leaders change the environment by simply walking into the room. Verse 32: "And when they climbed into the boat, the wind died down."

Apex Leaders allow God to tell his amazing story through their lives. Verse 33: "Then those who were in the boat worshiped him, saying, 'Truly you are the Son of God.'"

When I compare my leadership attempts to those of Jesus, I fall woefully short. Everyday I am reminded of the vast difference between Jesus and myself. It is only by his grace and what he did for me on the cross that I am worthy to lead anything. It is certainly not because of my competencies, background, experiences, or network.

Perhaps by learning more about him from Scripture and allowing him to live through my life, maybe I can become an even better leader—an Apex Leader worth following. How about you?

Personal and Group Discussion Questions

1. Would those you lead describe you as a servant leader or self-serving leader? Why?

2. What is the one sacrifice you made in the last year as a leader that benefited your team the most?

3. From the 13 lessons listed from Matthew 14:22-33 in this chapter, write down one lesson you can begin implementing TODAY to become a better leader.

CHAPTER 10
Apex Leaders Deliver Results

... Thou art worthy to take the book, and to open the seals thereof: for thou wast slain, and hast redeemed us to God by thy blood ... (Revelation 5:9, KJV)

I started writing this book by focusing on Jesus Christ. Lessons we can learn from him are sprinkled throughout the pages. It is only natural to conclude the final chapter by learning one more great lesson from him.

Jesus made every room he entered better. Jesus turned water into wine. He cleansed the temple from unethical business practices. He knew what people were thinking and then changed their perspectives. When Jesus asked a group of men to follow him, they did.

Jesus' teachings allowed people to be born again. He championed women's rights and gave people dignity. He changed the spiritual temperatures of entire cities. He healed the sick and raised the dead. He fed over 10,000 people with just five loaves of bread and two fish.

Jesus walked on water and also calmed raging seas just by saying, "Peace be still." He cast out demons and made people whole. Jesus was a scholar who won every debate he was ever in. He promised the Holy Spirit which would arrive in the book of Acts. And when it came to prayer, no one ever prayed like Jesus. In fact, after hearing him pray, one of his disciples approached him and requested, "Lord, teach us to pray."

Jesus attracted the largest crowds anyone had ever seen, yet he knew the number of hairs on every single head in those crowds. He valued children, the poor, widows, and the forgotten. Jesus gave everyone hope.

Jesus came to the defense of the defenseless. He gave sight to the blind. Jesus was the Good Shepherd. He washed feet and predicted his own death and resurrection. Jesus gave people a vision of who they could be and not just of who they were.

Jesus gave up all the blessings of heaven. He was then born in the form of a baby by virgin birth. Jesus never committed a sin. He took the punishment for all the sins committed by everyone in human history.

Jesus willingly gave up his life and died for our sins. Jesus also defeated hell and rose from the dead. He walked out of the tomb. He appeared to hundreds after his resurrection. He ascended into heaven. He is coming back for those who know him, and we will rule and reign with him forever.

Jesus is approachable enough for all to meet but whose ways we will never fully comprehend until we get to heaven.

On a personal note, Jesus Christ also changed my life. I am not the man I used to be.

This is just a small list of the things Jesus Christ did while on earth. Jesus delivered on everything he said he would do. Jesus delivered results.

Dr. John C. Maxwell, in his classic leadership book, *The 21 Irrefutable Laws of Leadership*, teaches The Law of Priorities which says a leader never confuses activity with accomplishment. Achieving results is one of the primary things separating Apex Leaders from all others. Did you get the job done? Benjamin Franklin once said, "He that is good for making excuses is seldom good for anything else."

In the summer of 2016, New York Yankees manager, Joe Girardi, gave one of the greatest examples of delivering results I have ever seen. Potential Hall of Famer Alex Rodriguez had announced his retirement mid-season and was hoping for a proper send-off which included some form of ceremony honoring his career.

After all, this is what basketball superstar Kobe Bryant had just received from the Los Angeles Lakers organization. But Girardi had other ideas. He kept Rodriguez on the bench and no ceremony was given.

Girardi's frustrations with the situation boiled over during a news conference. He said, "I'm not saying I don't think I can win with Alex in the lineup. What I'm saying is I'm putting out what I feel is the best lineup. That's my job. I mean that is in my job description. My job description does not entail farewell tours. My job description is to try to win every game and try to put everyone in the best possible position to do that. And that's what I'm trying to do." Girardi understood his job was to deliver winning results.

Joe Girardi would like Bill O'Brien. O'Brien, the head coach of the NFL's Houston Texans, said after benching his $72 million quarterback Brock Osweiler, "We don't make decisions about how much a guy gets paid. We make decisions on what's the best way to win a game." O'Brien also understood his job was to deliver winning results. As a leader, regardless of where you apply your talents, you have the same responsibility.

Apex Leaders Deliver Results

Tom Brady

Former NFL wide receiver Santana Moss famously said, "Big time players make big time plays in big time games." Few Apex Leaders have ever delivered better results in big time games than five-time Super Bowl champion quarterback Tom Brady. We can learn a lot from his habits because it is what allows him to perform at such a high level.

Delivering results requires preparation. Apex Leaders will either prepare or repair. Brady is winning before the ball is ever snapped. His preparation allows his pre-snap reads to understand everything the defense will do, and he then adjusts the offense appropriately.

Delivering results requires decisiveness. Apex Leaders like Brady do not suffer from confusion, lack of clarity, or passivity. He knows immediately where he wants to go with the ball and executes accordingly.

Delivering results requires talent. Apex Leaders maximize their natural abilities. Brady is not known for having a strong arm, but he takes full advantage of the skills he does have.

Delivering results requires you to limit unnecessary mistakes. One of Brady's greatest skills is how accurate he is with the ball. Apex Leaders limit

132

unforced errors.

For more on how Brady delivers results, let's hear from the man himself. The following comments and leadership lessons on delivering results come from an ESPN July 25th, 2015, interview. Notice how many of Brady's traits have already been mentioned in previous chapters.

Delivering results requires energy. The world is run by tired leaders. Fatigue is a leader's constant companion. Brady said, "The hard part about training camp is once you wear down it's hard to recover because you're at it six days a week."

To continually deliver results requires continual improvement. Brady is never satisfied with his current performance. He noted, "Every year has its challenges in different ways...you've always got to work on something."

Something few leaders realize is the source of their confidence. The confidence to successfully deliver results flows from a leader's memory. They have been there before. As Brady worked with younger members on the team, he realized, "That's the difference between a rookie year and a second year. Guys have done it, proved it, and now you have confidence going into the next season that we're actually good at some things. And those are the things you want to build on. "

A proper understanding of opportunity is also important in delivering results. There is a significant difference between sensing opportunity and seizing it. To deliver results, you must seize current opportunity. Brady said, "The most important [year] is this year, because that's all we have."

There is one thing which will stop a leader's ability to deliver results more than anything else. Believe it or not, it is his or her health. Once health is lost, a leader ceases to be effective. This is why a leader's greatest ability is their availability. Brady's long career is partly because of his passion for good health. He said, "... a lot of luck and a lot of great education from some really important people in my life that have taught me how to take care of myself, how to prepare myself mentally and physically for what we're up against. It's probably not what a lot of people do. It's probably not the norm for most players, but it's what's worked for me."

What else is not the norm is Brady's passion for the game. He remembered, "I made a commitment to myself because I love the game; I want to play for a long time. There's nothing else I'd rather do. I make a commitment in the season and the off-season to do that. It's a fun thing for me. It's not like working out is a very hard thing; coming out and playing football in the middle of May is a hard thing. I love doing it."

We have discussed a number of the reasons Brady has been able to deliver such superior results for such an extended period of time — preparation, decisiveness, talent, accuracy, energy, continual improvement, confidence, good health and passion. But there is one thing Brady and other leaders who deliver superior results have that average leaders simply do not possess.

Apex Leaders deliver superior results and execute under pressure. In the NFL Films documentary *The Brady 6*, Brady provided unique insight into the mind of Apex Leaders. He said, "To me, what separates really good players from great players — execute well under pressure. The biggest game. The biggest stage. That's what playing quarterback is all about."

Brady appeared on no bigger stages than Super Bowl XLIX against the Seattle Seahawks and Super Bowl LI against the Atlanta Falcons. During the fourth quarter and overtime against both teams, in the most pressure-packed environments a quarterback can be in, and facing the league's best defense (Seattle) and trailing by 25 points (Atlanta), Brady played his absolute best. He threw for a combined 34 completions in 43 attempts (81%), three touchdowns and zero interceptions in the two games. Tom Brady delivered results when it mattered most and has two additional Super Bowl trophies to show for it.

It is very educational to learn leadership lessons from athletes. After all, sports deal with talent evaluation, hard decisions, strategy, preparation, teamwork, coaching, hard work, sacrifice, performing under pressure, and learning how to deal with success and failure. A person's life does not depend on delivering results in the athletic arena, but it certainly does for the brave men and women serving in our armed forces.

Navy SEAL commander Rorke Denver said in his book, *Worth Dying For*, "Technical skill, creative thinking, clear vision, selflessness, team spirit, and strong leadership can all be honed with training and experience. The part we can't manufacture, the part you have to bring from home, is the character that keeps you going and the refusal to ever stop short of success."

Delivering results for Navy SEALs is not optional. Success or failure means life or death to them personally, their unit, and potentially many in our nation. This is why he adds, "Failure is not an option. It's not even an imaginable possibility."

Captain Chesley "Sully" Sullenberger
For airplane pilots, human lives are dependent on their ability to successfully complete their assignment as well. Their job is to get hundreds of people safely from Point A to Point B while traveling

in a metal tube at high speed, thousands of feet in the air.

William Langewiesche's book, *Fly By Wire: The Geese, The Glide, The Miracle Of The Hudson*, details the account of the January 15, 2009, US Airways flight piloted by Captain Chesley, "Sully," Sullenberger. After colliding with a flock of Canadian geese, Captain Sullenberger safely glided the plane to rest in the Hudson River saving all 151 lives onboard.

Justifiably, Captain Sullenberger has been viewed as an American hero. In fact, Tom Hanks portrayed the pilot and the events surrounding his successful water landing in the 2016 major motion picture, *Sully*. Langewiesche's book reminds us about the importance of delivering results.

Apex leaders often go unnoticed until they are needed to deliver superior results in a crisis. Captain Sullenberger's life was uneventful and went largely unnoticed even by his peers at US Airways until that January day. However, he had been preparing for this moment his entire career. Captain Sullenberger learned to fly in high school on a grass field and earned a private license at age 17. He also flew while at the Air Force Academy. In Captain Sullenberger's book, *Highest Duty*, the publisher notes that, "Sully believes his life experience prior to the emergency landing was a preparation for his success. And that life's greatest challenges can be met if we are ready for them."

To successfully deliver results you must have self-control. Once again, I am referring to the importance of self-leadership. As an expert and experienced pilot, Captain Sullenberger was capable of "intense mental focus and exceptional self-control." It should also be noted he rarely swears–another sign of self-control.

Experience and institutional knowledge are also critical to delivering results when they are needed the most. We live in a world quick to discount experience, but during times of crisis, pattern recognition is vital for success. When asked, "How do you think that your experience with over twenty thousand hours as a pilot helped you during this experience?" Captain Sullenberger answered, "It allowed me to focus clearly on the highest priorities at every stage of the flight, without having to constantly refer to the written guidance."

To successfully deliver results, you must be calm, confident, and creative. After years of flying, Captain Sullenberger had hit flocks of birds and experienced engine failure before. He was confident enough to immediately improvise and find flight solutions not taught in training rather than relying on by-the-book procedures. People are always a picture of their leader. They especially take their cues from the leader during crisis situations. The crew and cabin passengers reflected Captain Sullenberger's calm demeanor during the landing.

Langewiesche wrote regarding Captain Sullenberger's emotional state during the plane's forced water landing, "You fly the airplane first, you navigate second, you talk on the radio after that. Sullenberger was clear about the priorities. His silences were brilliant."

If you want to deliver superior results, it is important to narrow your focus. Captain Sullenberger also ruthlessly shed distractions as he approached the Hudson. Captain Sullenberger and Officer Skiles focused on only two things — getting the engines started and finding a place to land the plane. This requires decisiveness as a leader. Captain Sullenberger made the decision to turn back toward LaGuardia Airport only 18 seconds following the bird strike.

As we discussed in Chapter One, you cannot deliver superior results without having a great team around you. When asked why the landing went so well Captain Sullenberger said, "It was many things that in aggregate added up. Again, we had a highly experienced, well-trained crew. First Officer Jeff Skiles (co-pilot) and I worked well as a team."

Apex Leaders Deliver Results

Smart leaders understand you never get results at the expense of your people. After landing, Captain Sullenberger and Officer Skiles went through the cabin handing out life vests, directing passengers, and supervising the evacuation. Captain Sullenberger was the last one off the plane. He was also the last one off the life rafts into a ferry. Finally, he was the last one off the ferry.

Most importantly, successfully delivering results only occurs when your entire team and everyone you are called to serve as a leader wins. Everyone must cross the finish line. As previously mentioned, all 151 passengers and five crewmembers survived.

Once again, Captain Chesley, "Sully," Sullenberger is an American hero who delivered the type of results we will never forget.

Another place where delivering results affects people's lives is the local church. In fact, the leadership in the local church can have a positive or negative impact on a person's eternal destiny.

The purpose of leadership in a local church is to advance mission and vision. Leaders can take your ministry farther, faster. Unfortunately, some pastors and church leaders do not foster a leadership culture.

When new and existing leaders are not identified, engaged, and discipled, the results are tragic. The

Kingdom loses. The church loses. People lose. Families lose. The community loses. Businesses and local schools lose. Everyone loses.

The following are signs of a church leadership culture that will not produce positive results in the lives of people:

Pastors and church leaders do not prioritize building relationships with leaders. For example, is the pastor's calendar prioritized to spend time with leaders? Similar to Jesus, pastors feed the 5,000 (large group) on Sunday then spend time with the 12 (leaders) during the week.

Leaders are ignored. Their contribution is not appreciated. They are not consulted prior to key decisions being made. Few things are as disheartening to leaders as having their opinions discounted or marginalized.

Positions are not being created for leaders. Churches do a great job creating opportunities for people to serve with their hands and feet. Churches do a poor job creating opportunities for high-capacity, marketplace leaders to serve with their minds.

Entrepreneurial leadership is not celebrated. Leaders are forced to take their talents outside the church to live out their calling. Because of staff bureaucracy or lack of vision, the leaders are forced to bypass their very own church.

Leaders are not properly resourced. They are not given the tools, financial resources, or facilities needed to reach their full redemptive potential. Results are also not measured. Leaders care about their return on investment. They want their lives, time and financial resources to matter and make a difference to others. Other times, successful leaders are reigned in by insecure leaders when their areas of ministry become too successful.

There are also two groups of leaders that are routinely marginalized in a poor leadership culture: next generation leaders and women. Next generation leaders are overlooked. They are not identified and developed to lead in the future. Also, many churches never place women in key roles of influence except perhaps in the areas of hospitality, children's ministry, or worship arts.

The worst example of a church with a poor leadership culture is one where its leaders are not thanked for their contribution. They are taken for granted. This is the saddest of all.

Earlier in this book, we discussed Zacchaeus, the chief tax collector, who wanted to see Jesus. In this situation, Zacchaeus wasn't the only one who was looking for something. Jesus wanted something from

Zacchaeus as well. Jesus wanted a relationship with him. Not only did these two have a nice meal and wonderful time together, they are now spending all of eternity together. Both men achieved their desired results.

A leader's character and people skills make someone *want* to follow them. The ability to deliver results determines if someone actually *will* follow them. Your ability to grow in influence is directly connected to your ability to deliver results. Can you take a group of individuals successfully from Point A to Point B? Will you get the job done? People will naturally gravitate to the leader who can.

People want to follow a leader with a clear vision and a plan to achieve it. They want to follow someone who cares about them and will make their lives better. Followers want to get behind a decisive leader who brings solutions to the issues they face. They want to be part of a winning team.

Leaders of winning teams rise early, have high energy, continually learn, eliminate distractions, focus, and rely on God to produce superior results.

It has been said, "If you think you are leading but no one is following, you are merely taking a walk." Conversely, there are long lines of people following leaders who deliver results. Apply these principles, and you'll position yourself at the very front of the line — as the apex leader.

Personal and Group Discussion Questions

1. What is one leadership principle from the life of Jesus you learned in this book that would make you a better leader if implemented?

2. Are you currently spending time on "busy work" — tasks that do not add to your success? Write them down. Are you willing to delegate these tasks or eliminate them all together? Why or why not?

3. What are you doing to create a leadership culture in your organization?

Conclusion

When my daughter was four years old, we attended an event called "Walk Through Bethlehem." This was an outdoor presentation of the birth of Jesus performed during the Christmas season. We walked station-to-station where a different part of the story was told.

Our family rounded a corner, and waiting in the next booth was a beautifully illuminated angel announcing the birth of the Savior. It was magnificent. The angel's elevated position was statuesque. The white robe was beautiful. The lighting was overwhelming. The entire scene was truly majestic.

My young daughter said, "Wow dad, look at that! I have never seen anything so amazing!" With a sense of pride and simply wanting to take in this wonderful experience, I said, "I know sweetie! It's beautiful, isn't it?" It was then our Hallmark moment took a sharp turn.

She proclaimed with absolute joy, "I've never seen a goat that beautiful!" My daughter was missing the breathtaking angel announcing the birth of our Savior because she was looking at a goat.

Here's my point. The Bible is the greatest leadership

book ever written. Everything you need to experience success and growth as a leader can be found in God's Word. I hope this book has helped you see the principles taught in Scripture are being lived out all around you today.

If you want to be a leader who reaches the top of your profession, you must build a great team around you. You must humble yourself enough to know you cannot do it alone, and you have to continually improve because yesterday's methods will not solve today's problems.

After much hard work, you will begin forming mutually beneficial relationships. It is true one can put a thousand to flight, but two can put ten thousand to flight. Once you have a great team, it is humility, continual improvement, hard work and strategic partnerships that will make others better. Then you will be able to consistently serve others in a generous manner and serve as an example to everyone in your industry.

It is only this select group of leaders who have implemented the nine previous practices that can deliver superior results. These are the Apex Leaders, and the principles they live out are truly timeless. May you experience great success as you incorporate these practices into your leadership.